Conservation
A Beginner's Guide

ONEWORLD BEGINNER'S GUIDES combine an original, inventive, and engaging approach with expert analysis on subjects ranging from art and history to religion and politics, and everything in between. Innovative and affordable, books in the series are perfect for anyone curious about the way the world works and the big ideas of our time.

anarchism	forensic science
artificial intelligence	french revolution
the beat generation	history of science
biodiversity	humanism
bioterror & biowarfare	islamic philosophy
the brain	journalism
the buddha	lacan
censorship	life in the universe
christianity	machiavelli
civil liberties	mafia & organized crime
classical music	marx
cloning	medieval philosophy
cold war	middle east
crimes against humanity	NATO
criminal psychology	oil
critical thinking	the palestine–israeli conflict
daoism	philosophy of mind
democracy	philosophy of religion
dyslexia	philosophy of science
energy	postmodernism
engineering	psychology
evolution	quantum physics
evolutionary psychology	the qur'an
existentialism	racism
fair trade	the small arms trade
feminism	sufism

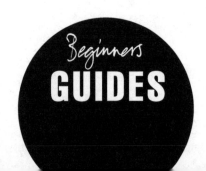

Conservation
A Beginner's Guide

Paul Jepson and Richard Ladle

ONEWORLD
OXFORD

A Oneworld Paperback Original

Published by Oneworld Publications 2010

ISBN 978–1–85168–714–5

Typeset by Jayvee, Trivandrum, India
Cover design by A. Meaden
Printed and bound in Great Britain by Bell & Bain, Glasgow

Oneworld Publications
UK: 185 Banbury Road, Oxford, OX2 7AR, England
USA: 38 Greene Street, 4th Floor, New York, NY 10013, USA
www.oneworld-publications.com

Learn more about Oneworld. Join our mailing list to
find out about our latest titles and special offers at:

www.oneworld-publications.com

Mixed Sources
Product group from well-managed
forests and other controlled sources
www.fsc.org   Cert no. TT-COC-002769
© 1996 Forest Stewardship Council

Contents

Acknowledgements   vii
Illustrations   ix

1 The scope of conservation   1

2 The conservation movement   11

3 Building influence   34

4 Science-based conservation   51

5 Taking action   82

6 Financing conservation   113

7 Conservation's critics   135

8 Twenty-first-century conservation   153

Further reading   175
Index   183

Acknowledgements

As individuals in the privileged position of teaching a Masters course on conservation at the University of Oxford we are continually amazed and heartened by the intellect, knowledge, commitment and the number of young people ready to pursue careers in conservation. This book was partly inspired by our experiences of teaching them. In addition it was inspired by the amazing people from all walks of life who commit their time, energy and imagination to conserving the natural world and who we have had the pleasure of meeting, working with and listening to. We are grateful to our friends and colleagues who have accompanied us on our conservation journeys over the years and in particular to fellow academics Bill Adams, Miguel Araújou, Andrew Barry, Lindsey Gillson, Steve Jennings, Jamie Lorimer, David MacDonald, Frans Vera, Kathy Willis.

This book would not have been possible without the input of many people who helped us to refine our ideas, read and commented on chapters and provided the encouragement needed for us to complete the manuscript in the midst of lectures, children, birding, fishing and other distractions. We would like to give special thanks to our editor Marsha Filion who instigated the project and retained faith through some early 'experimental' drafts and our copy-editor, Ann Grand, who finally beat the manuscript into shape. We would also like to thank our partners Susanne Schmitt and Ana Malhado for their encouragement, patience and insightful comments and suggestions during the writing process.

The book benefited immensely from suggestions on what should be excluded and included and from sections being read by a wide range of excellent scientists and conservationists. In particular we would like to thank: Tony Baker, Dan Brockington, Maan Barua, Hari Balasubramanian, Tessa Bergmann, Max Bokcoff, Paul Chatterton, Rob Coleman, Anna Cura, Georgina Domberger, Suzi Heaton, Jim Jarvie, Steve Jennings, Stephanie Hilbourne, Mike Ladle, Lillian Ladle, Martha Lang, Li Li, Dan Laffoley, Diana Mastracci, Paul Morling, Anton Oliver, Ed Perry, Mike Rands, Andrew Taber, Carolina Trevisi-Fuentis, Anni Vuhelainen, Jim Wardill, Chun Wong, Mark Wright, Robert Whittaker.

Our hope is that this book will provide an overview of modern conservation and aid and encourage anyone who cares for the natural world to get involved, not just as helpers for an existing conservation effort but as voices that will help shape how we do conservation in the twenty-first century.

Illustrations

Figure 1   Visiting natural areas helps to promote national pride and can make significant contribution to national and local economies. (photo © Paul Jepson)   4

Figure 2   The thylacine (Tasmanian tiger) was hunted to extinction by the mid 1930s   12

Figure 3   Caspar David Freidrich's early nineteenth century painting *Wanderer Above the Sea of Fog* captures the concept of the sublime, in which individual interaction with the grandeur of nature becomes an emotional and aesthetic act of self-fulfillment   16

Figure 4   William Beebe (left) and his bathysphere   21

Figure 5   Peter Scott and HRH Prince Philip at WWW International Headquarters in 1967, Les Uttins, Morges, Switzerland (photo © WWF Intl./WWF-Canon)   25

Figure 6   The structure of the Forest Stewardship Council (FSC)   46

Figure 7   The FSC logo – now seen on wood products from around the world   47

Figure 8   Extinction drivers   53

Figure 9   A 'medium-sized' Nile perch (photo © Mike Ladle)   60

Figure 10   Fogging (spraying trees with insecticide) is one of the main methods of discovering new species of insect in tropical forests (photo © Paul Jepson)   67

Figure 11   Structure of IUCN Red List categories   69

Figure 12   Traditionally, conservation organisations have trained students in techniques for taking wildlife censuses but building their capacity to understand how their peers value wildlife and the environment is just as important for successful conservation action. (photo © Fahrul P. Amama)   77

Figure 13   Millions of people depend on medicinal plants for basic health care. Conservation scientists work with indigenous experts, such as this Tibetan Yamche, to study the distribution and harvesting of medicinal plants to promote sustainable harvesting (photo © Susanne F. Schmitt)   79

Figure 14   Although the scale and impact of illegal logging are well-known, many countries still find it difficult to enforce their laws on the ground (photo © Paul Jepson)   80

Figure 15   A critical cartoon of 'big' conservation (*"Relax, we're from Conservation, Inc."* © *William Bramhal, reproduced with permission of the artist*)   142

Figure 16   Conservation's contribution to Maslow's hierarchy of human needs   150

Figure 17   A Dutch 'greenway' linking two fragmentary habitats (photo © rijkswaterstaat/joop) van Houdt Fotografie   155

Figure 18   The Oostvaaderplassen: letting nature take its course (photo © Vincent Wigbels)   168

1
The scope of conservation

One of conservation's most audacious initiatives is taking place in the Netherlands, one of the most densely populated areas of Western Europe. The Dutch have created a 'Serengeti behind the dykes'; a completely new sort of nature reserve, where some of Europe's extinct mammals have been 'recreated' and wander freely through grassland, glade and marsh. This is not a heritage safari park but the Oostvaarderplassen reserve, just a forty-minute drive from Amsterdam. This reserve is an example of the move away from human management and manipulation of a habitat to create a 'natural' state and towards a situation where the interactions between the animals and their habitat determines the nature 'produced'. The progressive Dutch ecologists behind the Oostvaarderplassen initiative want to restore the processes and flows that create living ecosystems and are little concerned with the traditional focus on conserving pristine landscapes, rare habitats and endangered species. This experiment presses the Western conservation movement to consider its purpose: should conservation be about restoring a pre-industrial nature or creating the conditions in which a 'new nature' can emerge amidst rapid social and environmental change?

Fundamentally, the Oostvaarderplassen experiment is prompting conservationists to ask what is meant by 'nature' and 'natural'. Before the spread of agriculture, Europe was home to a diversity of large herbivores, including wild horses, wild cattle, elk, bison and deer. The numbers of many of these animals are now greatly diminished; the auroch (wild cow) and tarpan (wild horse) have been officially extinct since 1627 and 1876 respectively. In truth, neither species was wiped out but was transformed to suit human needs; the Dutch are using specially bred horses and cattle to develop creatures that resemble the ancestral forms in appearance and behaviour – a process known as dedomestication. This is controversial: the Dutch animal welfare lobby was appalled when cows and horses (as they see them) were allowed to starve to death during a hard winter. The ecologist in charge of the reserve argued that this was inevitable and that during their life the animals experienced natural herd behaviour; something denied to their farmed relations.

Conservation is a cultural force that encourages societies to reflect upon and regulate their relationship with the non-human world. Approaches to conservation differ markedly between countries, depending on cultural attitudes, beliefs and traditions, familiar and iconic landscapes and wildlife, people's dependence on natural resources and the power of the conservation voice. Different societies have different moral, aesthetic and practical reasons for conserving nature and different ideas of the 'natural': for many North Americans, the word evokes images of the majestic landscapes of the American West; for Europeans, notions of the pastoral idyll; and for East Asians, an infusion of ideas of harmony and balance.

The concept of conservation may have diverse philosophical roots but a relatively small suite of causes define conservation. One is the saving of a rare species from looming extinction, such as the Chatham Island robin. At the start of the 1980s, this small black bird seemed a doomed species. The last five birds lived on a tiny outcrop of rock, Little Mangere Island, 800 kilometres east of New Zealand's South Island. Little Mangere was slowly being taken over by an invasive vine that was squeezing the life out of the habitat. In a last-ditch attempt to save the species, the remaining birds were captured by the New Zealand Wildlife

Service and taken to a slightly larger island, where the vines were less of a problem. To increase their reproduction rate, the first clutch of robin eggs laid every year was removed and placed in tomtit nests, who acted as surrogate parents for the critically endangered robins. Despite breeding within a restricted gene pool, the robin population has grown every year and although the species remains endangered, there are now over 250 robins and they are no longer considered to be at imminent risk of extinction.

Another notable cause, the canvas for globally popular wildlife television programmes, is the protection of places where human populations are small. One of the most spectacular examples of such a wilderness is the Ngorongoro Conservation Area (NCA), in the highlands of Tanzania. At the heart of the NCA is the Ngorongoro crater, the world's largest unflooded caldera. The NCA has the highest density of mammalian carnivores in Africa and is a magnet for tourists and the setting for countless television documentaries. However, conspicuously missing from nearly all of these documentaries are the native inhabitants of the area – the Maasai. It is perhaps unsurprising that the Maasai do not feature strongly in the conservation narrative; they did not move into the NCA until 1959, having been forcibly evicted from the nearby Serengeti National Park. However, even this move proved temporary, as in 1974 they were evicted from the fertile grounds in the centre of the crater because the economic reality was (and largely still is) that it is the large mammals that bring in the tourists, who are generally uninterested in looking at other humans, even if they are one of the last tribes on the planet.

A third conservation concern, which has attracted considerable public attention, is the fight to stop unnecessary and wanton slaughter. The campaigns of middle-class Victorian ladies against the fashion for wearing bird plumes, the heroic efforts of 1970s Greenpeace activists against commercial hunting of whales and current efforts to curtail the hunting of primates for bushmeat are three of many examples in which conservationists have pressed governments, businesses and citizens to put wildlife before easy profit.

These three emblematic causes capture just a fraction of the agendas and activities of contemporary conservation. Modern conservationists have a broad and complex remit, which includes trying to reduce the impact on the natural world of markets, poverty, population growth, development, climate change and other human-induced conditions. This book is about the challenges of conservation in the modern globalised world and the varied, often ingenious, ways in which conservationists are meeting them. The biggest challenge is – perhaps surprisingly – not global warming or habitat loss (although they

Figure 1 Visiting natural areas helps to promote national pride and can make significant contributes to national and local economies (photo © Paul Jepson)

are areas of great concern) but how to maintain influence in a world in which traditional forms of government are rapidly being replaced by devolved governments, market mechanisms and networks of transnational agents, including inter-governmental organisations, multi-national corporations and charities. In this 'brave new world' of savvy consumers and diminishing public funds, conservation can no longer rely on traditional, top-down 'command and control' politics and must fight to be heard by developing a host of exciting new strategies with which to address its diverse audiences.

One of those strategies is to bring conservation in line with international agendas on sustainable development and the allevi-ation of poverty. Nowadays, conservation is no longer just about protecting landscapes because of their intrinsic worth, as places for outdoor recreation, the study of ecological systems or symbols of natural cultural identity. Rather, its purpose is to maintain the ecological services, such as clean water, erosion control and crop pollination, on which human societies depend or to provide new development and economic activity for local people. These can be achieved through better marketing and management of natural resources, promotion of ecotourism or limited commercialisation of plant and animal resources.

Another strategy is to work with businesses to create incen-tives to protect habitats or encourage their sustainable manage-ment. This approach has been used in several major initiatives, for example where conservationists team up with other social developments such as the organic farming and Fairtrade® movements. The success of this strategy is evident on the super-market shelves of the Western world, whose products display eco-labels and other claims of wildlife and environmental friend-liness. Such efforts bring conservation on to the High Street and into people's lives. The conservation organisations that employ and promote these approaches are leading a 'quiet revolution' in how companies and markets view the environment.

Oil and mining companies now endorse a strategy of no net loss of biodiversity, which they hope to achieve by a combination of careful operation, habitat restoration and the offsetting of the impact of their operations. These companies are setting up projects to save habitats that would otherwise be lost because they realise that investing in conservation could be in their long-term interest. Such investment mitigates the risks of damaging campaigns by conservation activists, helps companies recruit and retain the best staff and makes it easier to secure the licenses and monies that they need to operate. Leading investment houses have responded to this trend towards green consumerism by launching a raft of 'socially responsible investment' products that enable individuals and institutions to make decisions that reflect their social and environmental beliefs. This could create a virtuous circle and change the way businesses and markets relate to the natural world.

A third strategy, albeit possibly an unconscious one, is for conservation to remain responsive to wider themes in popular culture and science: seen, for example, in the growing popularity of species reintroduction and habitat restoration. These activities chime with an eclectic mix of trends and interests ranging from the popularity of television 'makeover' programmes to public participation in debates on genetic engineering and cloning; from the enduring appeal of science fiction to a deep love of gardening. Such endeavours enrich our lives without costing the Earth. Consider, for example, the hugely successful reintroduction of the red kite to south-east England in the 1980s. Probably, the majority of the twenty million or so inhabitants of the south-east had never heard of the red kite nor knew of its extermination during the seventeenth century (by the late twentieth century only a small remnant population of these birds survived in isolated Welsh valleys). Now, through conservationists' efforts, the dreary motorway commute from Oxford to London is enlivened by groups of kites soaring overhead, walkers in the Chilterns' Area of Outstanding Natural Beauty enjoy the sight of these beautiful birds and residents of rural areas can bring drama to their bird tables by putting out the carcass of their Sunday lunch! The red kite introduction project has added a little extra something to people's lives and helped keep nature and the conservation cause in the public's consciousness.

Species such as the red kite, the white-tailed sea eagle and the timber wolf have been brought back primarily for aesthetic and cultural reasons. The driving forces behind such reintroductions are the thrill of seeing magnificent animals and the making of a tangible connection with our species' history. In the future humanity's longing to bring back lost animals may not be limited to restoring those that have been lost from the local area but are still abundant in other regions. In November 2008, researchers at Pennsylvania State University in the USA announced that they had decoded almost all the genetic information of the woolly mammoth, from the frozen 60,000-year-old remains found in Siberia. Dr Stephan Schuster, who led the research team, said in the *Daily Telegraph* (UK) that the research represented a major step in the quest to 'bring back an extinct species that modern humans have missed meeting by only a few thousand years'. Intriguingly, if the genetic engineers succeed, there is a good chance that the mammoth could be inserted into a waiting ecosystem: radical Russian ecologists have embarked on an Oostvaarderplassen-like project (dubbed Pleistocene Park) to restore the lost grasslands of Siberia by removing the pine forests and reintroducing the 'lost' large herbivore assemblage of musk ox, tarpan, reindeer and bison.

Conservation is a dynamic and eclectic cultural force, responsive to threats, opportunities, trends and ideas. Since the emergence of the modern conservation movement at the end of the nineteenth century, the demands placed on the natural world by human society have become ever more complex, far-reaching and severe. Perhaps the only constants are the unrelenting erosion of the diversity, abundance and extent of nature and the desire of people to do something about it.

Our aim is to explain the ways conservationists build and exert their influence in the modern world and to give the millions of people who donate to conservation causes a better idea of why their money is needed and on what it is spent. We want to provide a concise overview of the scope of conservation and the main areas of work for those planning to volunteer for conservation projects or embark on a career in conservation. Increasingly, conservation is pursued through partnerships with a range of supportive agencies and businesses: we hope to help those from other walks of life sympathetic to conservation to understand the modern agenda and identify areas of synergy and mutual interest. Finally, we hope that this overview will prompt conservation-minded people everywhere to take stock and engage in discussion about the aims and purposes of conservation. In Chapter 2, we introduce the origins of conservation and the organisations that drive the movement. In Chapter 3, we review how the conservation lobby has built its influence with governments and markets and created the frameworks for international and local action. Such has been its success that the question is not so much 'should we conserve nature?' but 'what should we conserve, how much do we need to protect and what species, habitats and regions should be our priority?' To maintain its influence and credibility, the conservation movement needs to provide timely and authoritative responses to these questions. In Chapter 4 we review the science of conservation, focusing on the fundamental questions of how science and technology can be used to monitor the state of nature and identify future problems. In Chapter 5, we introduce the main areas of direct action, focusing on conservation's three enduring pillars: establishing and governing protected areas, conserving species and managing habitats.

By this point, two things will be apparent: first, the practice of conservation is complex, costly and driven by private organisations; second, a small group of international conservation organisations have become dominant in shaping conservation's global objectives and practice. We address these points in Chapters 6 and 7, with an exposition of how conservation is financed and a review of the critiques of conservation by groups concerned with social justice and political accountability. We conclude our introduction to the world of conservation in Chapter 8, looking at trends that will shape conservation in the twenty-first century.

This book might leave you wondering where the boundaries of conservation lie and how it differs from the environmental movement or relates to animal welfare concerns. There is a considerable overlap but in our view, environmentalism is more human-centred in its motivations, concerned with maintaining a sound environment and equity in the distribution of environmental benefits and costs. The environmental movement embraces 'brown' issues, relating to pollution, toxins, waste disposal and resource extraction, and engages with the major industries whose activities affect the environment, for example energy, transport, agriculture, fisheries and forestry. In contrast, conservation is more closely aligned with 'green' issues: the protection and restoration of species, sites and habitats. Human-centred arguments are very much in the ascendancy but the conservation movement retains a strong belief that humans have moral responsibilities for the non-human world and that the aesthetic and intellectual contemplation of nature enriches human culture.

Conservation attends to the welfare of plants and animals but is primarily concerned with the relationship between society and nature. In contrast, the animal welfare movement focuses on how humans treat, and relate to, animals. Animal welfare and conservation are often seen as two aspects of the same concept:

a concern and compassion for the non-human world. Professional conservationists argue for a clearer distinction and distance themselves from actions that could be seen as sentimentalising or anthropomorphising animals. Primate rehabilitation centres are a high-profile activity in which many conservationists seek to stress the distinction. They argue that while an individual orang-utan or chimpanzee might benefit from being returned to the forest, there is little evidence to suggest that they can integrate back into wild primate groups and even less to suggest that such centres maintain the level of support needed to address the threats of deforestation and illegal capture – the main reasons why primates need to be rescued.

Such debates are healthy, indeed essential, if conservation is to remain a vibrant cultural force. It is important that arguments about what nature is, what we should conserve and why and who makes such decisions return to public debate. Climate change has recently re-established the environment as a mainstream political and media issue. While this creates an exciting opportunity to re-examine our relationship with the natural world, the over-arching seriousness of climate change might also marginalise discussion and action relating to the fate of species and natural areas. In providing a guide to the mechanics of conservation, we hope that we can enable concerned citizens to engage more effectively.

2

The conservation movement

For Professor Bill Adams (Moran Professor of Conservation and Development, University of Cambridge), 'Conservation is never anything but social and never anything but political'. Conservation is the expression of people's desire to preserve the elements of the natural world that they value. For some, 'value' is as simple as economic worth; others are driven by moral concerns or an appreciation of nature's aesthetics. Some want to preserve because the natural world is beautiful, awe-inspiring or amazing. To some, nature is a God-given trust, bringing with it a religious duty to be good stewards of the Earth. For others, nature is full of precious resources that need to be nurtured and protected so future generations may use and enjoy them.

The expression of these diverse values is seen in the different approaches of modern conservation organisations, which are united by a desire to protect and restore the Earth's species and habitats but distinguished by their different values, strategies and memberships. Government bodies and smaller groups play a role but it is household names such as the WWF, Conservation International, the Royal Society for the Protection of Birds (RSPB), the Wildlife Conservation Society and the Nature Conservancy that are defining the agenda for twenty-first century conservation. These organisations make tangible the conservation values of society and have been responsible for many of the success stories of recent times.

To understand modern conservation practices, we must understand what the major conservation organisations stand for, where they came from and how they exert their influence. We begin here by describing conservation's organisational landscape and the phases of its development. In Chapter 3, we will explain how these organisations, through collaborations with governments and corporations, have secured conservation's place in government operations and markets and have exerted real influence in the pursuit of their conservation goals.

The origins of conservation

Modern conservation groups, and the movement to which they belong, have relatively shallow historical roots. The earliest recognisably modern conservation organisations were founded in the cities of Europe and the east coast of America in the late

Figure 2 The thylacine (Tasmanian tiger) was hunted to extinction by the mid 1930s

nineteenth and early twentieth centuries, partly in response to the revolution in western thought concerning the human relationship with nature that was prompted by the publication of Charles Darwin's *On the Origin of Species* in 1859. At the beginning of the nineteenth century, most people considered humans to have been created by God in His image, that nature's bounty was inexhaustible and that only God could destroy what He had created. This perception was transformed by a series of influential discoveries, events and circumstances that provoked a vigorous debate about this relationship, such as a sudden and well-publicised rash of extinctions including the great auk (1852), the passenger pigeon (1914) and the thylacine (1936), the rapid demise of the vast forests of the American Great Lakes region and the discovery of the great apes (the first scientific description of a gorilla came in 1847) with anatomy clearly very similar to our own.

For many in the West, the belief that nature is a robust, pre-ordained system was replaced by the realisation (or possibility) of the fragility of natural systems and the divine creation of humans by a recognition of our close kinship with other animals. Intense public debate surrounded this changing worldview and leading thinkers began to articulate new ideals and aspirations for how humanity should relate to the non-human world. Some were motivated by a desire to reassert the uniqueness of human identity – extending the human qualities of compassion, morality and respect for others was a sure way of setting humans apart from the rest of life on Earth. Others took a more pragmatic approach and promoted values of wise management and use of natural resources to avoid shortages that would compromise future human development.

The impact of these shifts in thinking varied among different professions and interest groups and in different cities and cultures. In Europe, the legacies of two cultural movements – natural history's focus on the naming and classifying of species and romanticism's exploration of the aesthetic and emotional feelings generated by wild nature – gave rise to the idea that artistic and scientific contemplation of nature is part of a shared cultural heritage. Social activists working to improve the health of London's poor framed a relationship with nature couched in terms of the benefits of healthy outdoor recreation and the need to protect 'green lungs' in and around cities. In North America, whose intellectuals focused on throwing off the yoke of colonialism and creating a distinct cultural identity, the emphasis was on conserving 'pristine' landscapes as wildernesses where people could feel closer to God. Elsewhere in the world, the influential community of scientists in the vital colonial forestry and agricultural industries promoted down-to-earth values concerning the rational and planned use of nature.

The point we want to stress is that this tumultuous recasting of the human–nature relationship set the scene for the formulation of distinct, yet complementary, social values. Many conservation groups can trace their roots to organisations formed to promote one or more of these values (aesthetic, utilitarian, religious and so on) but most supported or embraced others. Groups of citizens on either side of the Atlantic mobilised to follow new conservation agendas that chimed with their cultural background, interests and social schemes. The fundamental values of the conservation movement and the distinct interest groups or social movements associated with it are summarised in Table 1. These values flowed easily between groups and prominent individuals around the world, due to the Victorian passion for letter-writing that linked extended families in Europe and America with the colonies of Asia and Africa.

In the latter half of the twentieth century, the relative emphasis given to these different social values changed. Some were transformed in the light of new knowledge, and new ones were added. The publication in 1962 of Rachel Carson's seminal book *Silent Spring* made explicit the direct impact of

Table 1 Fundamental social values of conservation

Social value	Movement and date	Leaders
Access to nature and countryside is necessary for the health and well-being of urban-dwellers. Free enjoyment of nature is one of humanity's most precious privileges and should not to be abridged by private right for greed or gain.	**Open-spaces movement** London, mid-19th century New York, early 20th century	Social reformers and urban planners
Healthy ecosystems are necessary to safeguard economic growth, quality livelihoods and social stability. Natural resources should be managed for the greatest good for the greatest number in the long term.	**Wise-use movement** British colonies, 18th century US, early 20th century	Government and university scientists
Landscapes evoking wilderness should be preserved as a benchmark from which to assess urban-industrial modernity and as places for spiritual, aesthetic and physical exploration and rejuvenation.	**Wilderness movement** California, late 19th century	Artists and writers
Human conquest of nature carries with it a moral responsibility to ensure the survival of threatened life forms. Wanton and unnecessary slaughter of wildlife is cruel.	**Wildlife movement** New York, late 19th century London, early 20th century	Big-game hunters, politicians and entrepreneurs
Aesthetic and intellectual contemplation of nature are integral to the biological and cultural inheritance of many peoples and monuments of nature should be guarded from ruin.	**Nature monument movement** Western European cities, early 20th century	Natural historians and other prominent citizens

Figure 3 Caspar David Freidrich's early nineteenth century painting *Wanderer Above the Sea of Fog* captures the concept of the sublime, in which individual interaction with the grandeur of nature becomes an emotional and aesthetic act of self-fulfillment

agricultural toxins on human health and prompted the emergence of values relating to environmental justice: the idea that both environmental risks (for example, pollution) and environmental benefits (for example, clean water) should be equally distributed throughout society without discrimination. Similarly, concerns about population growth and depletion of resources motivated the landmark Stockholm Conference on the Human Environment in 1972. At this conference, the value of inter-generational equity was fully articulated: the responsibility of humanity to protect and improve the environment for present and future generations.

Conservation is not a single cause but a collection of social values and agendas that seek both to protect species and natural areas and, more generally, to govern our relationship with the natural world. Different values are expressed in different ways in different countries, among different groups and at different levels of government. Internationally, governmental values that stress the usefulness of nature to economic development and the alleviation of poverty have the greatest influence. At the national level, values that link nature conservation with national cultural identity are more likely to promote action. At the personal level, it is perhaps values relating to aesthetics and compassion for wildlife that motivate support for conservation. The challenge for conservation organisations, especially those with an international reach, is to tailor their arguments and agendas to specific audiences so as to have a powerful voice in living rooms, boardrooms and council chambers across the world.

The first conservation organisations

The first conservation organisations were established at the turn of the twentieth century. Early conservationists were typically active citizens, with a passion for protecting nature. They eagerly formed committees and societies but many had established careers and busy lives and so – with the exception of a few scientists, members of the aristocracy and leisured middle-class ladies – lacked the time, and perhaps the inclination, to devote all their energies to the conservation cause. These early conservationists can be grouped into three types: élite clubs and societies, made up of prominent citizens, able to deliver their agenda through the influence of their professional positions and networks; societies that employed professionals to promote new legislation and/or acquire land for conservation; and zoos, museums and botanic gardens.

The first category arguably includes the two most influential organisations in the history of the conservation movement. The first was established in 1887, by Theodore (Teddy) Roosevelt, who later became the twenty-sixth President of the United States of America. Following the (unrelated) deaths of his wife and mother on the same day in February 1884, he sought solace on his isolated ranch in North Dakota. For two years, he hunted, wrote and reflected on the devastation hunters and settlers were causing to the wildlife about which he was so passionate. During this time, he articulated the views that humans have a moral responsibility to save threatened species and that needless slaughter of wildlife is cruel and barbaric. On his return to New York, he formed the Boone and Crockett Club (B&CC) to start realising these values. The club had two goals: first, to create sanctuaries and refuges where wildlife could survive the onslaught of human expansion into frontier lands, and second, to change the culture of hunting to exalt the noble qualities of the chase above the number of animals killed.

The B&CC was truly an élite club; its one hundred members were leading political, business and media figures in New York and a condition of their membership was that they had hunted at least three of America's big game species. This strategy might sound preposterously *macho* today but it gave the club a huge influence. These men were shaping America; by promoting a new ethos and deriding those who were uncaring about the fate of wildlife or hunters who bragged about the number of animals they had shot, they helped bring wildlife issues to public attention and drive a dramatic change in the public's attitude to the natural world.

The activities of the B&CC inspired European big-game hunters to follow suit. In 1903, the Society for Preservation of the Wild Fauna of the Empire (SPWFE) was founded in London. The SPWFE drew its membership exclusively from the upper echelons of the British Empire. Its members were eminent men and included the Secretary of State for the Colonies, colonial governors and members of the House of Lords. The SPWFE shared many of the B&CC's concerns but its focus was the declining game populations in the colonies, particularly in Africa. In the early decades of the twentieth century, the two organisations joined forces to create the first international conservation treaty – the 1933 London Convention for the Protection of African Fauna and Flora – which created the legal basis for and had the political clout necessary to establish the network of parks that has saved Africa's wonderful wildlife from the threat of extinction and enriched global culture. The B&CC and SPWFE did not need to employ professionals to put pressure on high-level officials or raise money to buy land – their ranks contained the ambassadors needed for the diplomatic groundwork and the colonial governors who had the power to decide on land use in their territories. One hundred years on, after several transformations, the SPWFE has become Fauna and Flora International (www.fauna-flora.org).

The B&CC left its organisational legacy in its founding of the Zoological Society of New York. This society was an example of the third type of early conservation organisation: zoos, museums and botanic gardens. These organisations emerged in response to public and scientific interest in natural curiosities and the desire to find out more about the medicinal and agricultural value of plants and animals. Nowadays, most have a strong conservation remit, which can be traced to the founding of the New York society. Perhaps because they were so close to the apex of power, the leaders of the B&CC were pragmatic about the possibility of the success of their efforts to save America's mega-fauna. As insurance, they decided that the society's flagship would be a new type of zoo (built in 1896 in the Bronx) that would be an 'Ark' for endangered species. The Zoo's first major project was the captive breeding and restocking of the American West with bison, whose formerly vast herds of 60–100 million animals had been reduced to around 1,000 individuals. In 1993, the Zoological Society became the *Wildlife Conservation Society* (WCS) to better reflect its extensive engagement in field conservation projects. Today, the Wildlife Conservation Society is the world's fourth-largest conservation organisation, employing over 1,000 staff and with an annual turnover in excess of US$100 million.

A widespread strategy used by early conservationists to exert influence was to create organisations that were able to employ professional expertise, legally purchase land and become a public

WILLIAM BEEBE: CONSERVATION'S FIRST CELEBRITY SCIENTIST

Born in 1877, William Beebe arguably ranks as history's most influential conservation scientist. He was recruited at 22 years old, to be Director of Birds and worked for the Bronx Zoo for fifty-three years until he retired as Director of Research at the age of 75. He did pioneering work in the fledgling field of conservation biology and revolutionised public interest in tropical nature.

Beebe studied the animals and ecosystems of remote regions and communicated the results of his research and adventures in popular books, magazine articles, public lectures and later, radio talks. Beebe's compelling blend of nature, science, exotic locations and adventure made him a celebrity who moved easily in New York's literary, film and artistic circles. As a scientist, he helped transform natural history from a 'collect and catalogue' descriptive science to a study of the dynamic relationships between species. He led the first scientific expeditions to the Galapagos and established the first tropical research stations where scientists could study living rainforests in

WILLIAM BEEBE: CONSERVATION'S FIRST CELEBRITY SCIENTIST (*cont.*)

Figure 4 William Beebe (left) and his bathysphere

depth. Towards the end of his career, he began to study animal behaviour and helped lay the foundations for the discipline of ethology, famously developed by the European scientists Konrad Lorenz (who visited Beebe's field station) and Nico Tinbergen.

Driven by huge curiosity and spirit, Beebe was a daring explorer. He is best known for his cramped descents to the depths of the oceans in a bathysphere. In 1932, while half a mile down, he described the weird fauna seen from his porthole in a live radio broadcast heard simultaneously on NBC in the US and the BBC in the UK. He was also a great supporter and mentor to young talent – he helped launch Rachel Carson's career. Beebe's legacy runs through most of modern conservation and his ethos of rigorous field science is at the heart of the Wildlife Conservation Society. Moreover, his media-friendly mix of exotic nature, science and adventure has become a global model for engaging people with conservation.

rallying point. Some of the first dedicated conservation organisations modelled themselves on the societies that had been formed to abolish slavery and prevent cruelty to animals. In the UK, these organisations worked with Members of Parliament (who were often trustees) to create Private Members' bills that enshrined the agendas of the societies in law. They employed lawyers and analysts to draft bills, and to compile testimonies and evidence, and sought the support of other politicians. Once a bill was passed, their expertise was directed to helping ministers to flesh out the detailed implementation of regulations and monitor and cajole lower-level bureaucratic staff into getting things done.

This approach was adopted by activists of the 'open spaces' movement. In 1865, the Footpaths and Commons Preservation Society, sometimes called the world's first environmental group, was formed to campaign against a proposal to build houses on Hampstead Heath, whose fine airy views were hugely popular with day-trippers seeking respite from London's polluted factories and streets. It succeeded in rescuing the Heath from development and was also instrumental in preserving other London landmarks, such as Wimbledon Common and Epping Forest. The Footpaths and Commons Preservation Society, through its promotion of urban green space in city planning, has had a profound and lasting influence on the lives of city-dwellers throughout the world.

Other organisations were dedicated to buying land. This was particularly popular among groups who believed that outstanding natural sites are part of a society's scientific, artistic and cultural heritage and should be guarded from destruction. A good example is the Dutch conservation organisation, *Natuurmonumenten*, formed in 1905 by naturalists living in Amsterdam. The initial single aim of *Natuurmonumenten* was to protect the Naardermeer, a beautiful wetland on the outskirts of the city, threatened with development. From these rather narrow origins, the organisation has grown. It now owns 345 nature reserves in Holland, employs over 300 staff and has an annual turnover of around 75 million. In the UK, the National Trust, founded in 1895 by three Victorian philanthropists, used a Private Members' bill in 1907 to secure an Act of Parliament (the National Trust Act) that grants the organisation the right to buy and hold land in perpetuity for public benefit. The National Trust is now the UK's second largest landowner (after the Crown) and has a membership of over 3 million.

The broad objectives of early conservation organisations – influencing legislation, securing and managing land, managing collections of endangered species, monitoring progress and building the necessary political and public support – remain the core rationales for most conservation organisations. However, as we will see in Chapter 3, the range of activities and the professional expertise needed to deliver these objectives has mushroomed as the world has become more complex.

The new world order: the rise of governmental conservation

In the decades following the Second World War, the tactics of conservation changed. In the creation of the United Nations (1945) and the granting of independence to former colonies, leading figures saw an opportunity to integrate conservation into the architecture of the new world order and the administrative structures of newly independent nations. Their goal was to encourage governments to take on the job of conserving species and natural areas. Central to this objective was the creation of an inter-governmental organisation concerned with nature conservation. In 1947, the leaders of the European and US conservation networks convinced Sir Julian Huxley, Director of the newly formed United Nations Scientific, Education and Cultural Programme (UNESCO), to host a conference to discuss the establishment of such an organisation. The result was the International Union for the Protection of Nature (IUPN), created in 1948. In 1956, the IUPN changed its name to the International Union for the Conservation of Nature and Natural Resources (IUCN), to reflect the importance of the utility of nature in international affairs.

The formation of the IUPN placed conservation firmly on the global political agenda of the post-war new world order. This had two interesting repercussions: first, many newly independent countries saw conservation as an area of international policy in which they could assume leadership roles (it is in this context that the hosting of the 1969 IUCN general assembly in India, and the launch of 'Project Tiger' by President Indira Ghandi can be understood). Second, it made conservation a legitimate recipient of international development funds. Membership of the new global bureaucracy gave IUCN the remit to formulate international policy agendas and to issue best-practice guidelines.

In the 1970s, a crucial item on the IUCN agenda was to establish a world-wide network of natural reserves that encompassed the variety of species, habitats and systems found on Earth. Nowadays referred to as the 'representation principle', this was a wonderfully unifying agenda, which catered for the sustainable use elements favoured by the new breed of conservation technocrats while also embracing older conservation arguments based on moral or aesthetic concerns. Armed with this principle, the IUCN and other international agencies developed partnerships with the governments of developing countries to prepare national conservation plans and expand reserve networks. This gave impetus and rationale for governments to create, redefine or expand conservation departments.

This phase of international action – the creation of governmental conservation bodies – was a necessary pre-condition to the creation of the international frameworks and institutions needed for global conservation action. If individual governments lacked conservation departments, they would be reluctant to sign up to new international conservation agreements; or if they did, their agreement would be meaningless in practice. These fledgling government conservation agencies also provided the opportunity for Western conservation organisations to offer technical support, advice and funding – extending their international reach without overly offending national sensibilities.

WWF: the creation of a modern conservation organisation

By 1960, the fledgling global conservation movement was floundering, because the IUCN was running out of money. In

Figure 5 Peter Scott and HRH Prince Philip at WWF International Headquarters in 1967, Les Uttins, Morges, Switzerland (photo © WWF Intl./WWF-Canon)

that year, writing in the *Observer*, Julian Huxley gave a bleak assessment of the future of conservation. This prompted a committee of prominent citizens to come to the rescue and form one of the best-known global conservation organisations, the World Wildlife Fund (now referred to simply by the initials WWF).

Led by Peter Scott – son of the legendary Robert Falcon Scott (Scott of the Antarctic) – the WWF committee drafted a manifesto that declared it would 'create a professional organisation to raise the money needed to put the world-wide conservation movement on a proper footing'. The manifesto was signed by sixteen of the world's leading conservationists. At its launch, in 1961, Prince Bernhard of the Netherlands agreed to be the new organisation's President, while in the UK, HRH Prince Philip and in the USA, former President Dwight D. Eisenhower launched national appeals. The committee was far ahead of its time in its clear understanding of the importance of the media. Scott used his artistic talent to create the now-famous panda logo and WWF convinced the *Daily Mirror* newspaper to publish a special 'shock issue' in the week after its launch. This appeal received an unprecedented public response: £45,000 (about £2 million in today's money) poured in from readers. WWF was up and running.

WWF was conceived as a relatively straightforward fundraising and grant-giving body; the IUCN's professional staff and networks were to advise it on what projects to fund, help supervise their implementation and assess their impact. However, WWF soon transformed itself from a funding body to the major global player in conservation policy and delivery. This change was partly driven by the employment of 'representatives' in countries in which WWF supported a number of conservation projects. These representatives were more than administrators and managers; they helped field staff to negotiate complex local politics by getting to know key government officials, ambassadors and resident staff of other international agencies. They rapidly became the people with the knowledge and connections needed to work with governments in building national conservation strategies.

THE 1980 WORLD CONSERVATION STRATEGY

The influential British conservationist Max Nicholson, a co-founder of WWF, was a top-level civil servant, who relished politics and administration and believed strongly that the needs of conservation should be integrated into the planning of economic development. He was one of many influential voices arguing for the wise use of nature against those who believed that strict protection was the only strategy likely to ensure the long-term survival of the world's remaining large mammals. In 1972, Nicholson arranged a high-level meeting of international conservation and development organisations in Rome. This first step in integrating conservation and development was taken further by the UN Conference on the Human Environment, held in Stockholm in 1972, which led to the formation of the United Nations Environmental Programme (UNEP). UNEP then financed the IUCN in producing a World Conservation Strategy in collaboration with WWF.

The strategy, launched in 1980, was the first major conservation document that explicitly put humans at the centre of conservation. Its opening statement read 'the chief impediment to sustainable development is lack of conservation' and defined conservation as 'the management of human use of the biosphere and of the species that compose it, so that they may yield the greatest sustainable benefit to present generations while maintaining their potential to meet the need and aspirations of future generations'. The strategy stated that in the international realm the conservation agenda was to make development more sustainable. It consolidated the ascendancy of conservation's wise-use value arguments over the earlier moral and aesthetic arguments.

The birth of big conservation

Almost all big conservation organisations have been accused of 'neo-colonialism' – the imposition of Western values and culture on developing countries. The need to become more representative became more urgent in the run-up to the 1992 Earth Summit in Rio de Janeiro, attended by 172 government leaders and 2400 NGOs (most focused on development). At this summit, developing countries started to demand more control over local conservation agendas and natural resources. The old model of Western expatriate conservationists advising developing world governments looked increasingly outdated.

WWF responded to the new cultural climate by re-forming its country offices into independent organisations, governed by a local board of trustees and predominantly staffed by local people. WWF became a global network in which donor WWFs (located in richer Western countries) supported local projects implemented by other organisations in the WWF 'family'. Now, WWF International, whose headquarters are in Switzerland, provides overall co-ordination, leads network strategy development and manages programme offices in the few countries not yet deemed ready for an independent WWF organisation.

BirdLife International pioneered an alternative model, at the opposite end of the organisational spectrum to WWF. BirdLife was founded in 1922, as the International Council for Bird Preservation. As recently as the early 1980s, it had just a handful of staff, working in a tiny office in Cambridge, UK. Its rise to international prominence was initiated when its leaders devised the compelling proposition of forming an international partnership, under a single name, with national, bird-orientated conservation organisations. This strategy was immensely popular and in 1993, BirdLife International came into being. None of these organisations had the capacity to be global conservation players but collectively, they had a strong voice and image in international policy negotiations and could gain access to international development funds, develop joint projects and share data and resources.

THE RISE OF BIODIVERSITY

Since the late 1980s, the main focus of conservation has been the protection of the world's biological diversity, often shortened to the more user-friendly 'biodiversity'. Biodiversity refers to the variation of life on Earth at all levels of biological organisation, although for historical and practical reasons this is normally expressed in terms of genetic diversity, species and ecosystems. The term 'biodiversity' was coined as a way of making politicians and bureaucrats aware of looming extinction crises, particularly in the tropics. It quickly rose in prominence and was cemented in international policy at the 1992 Earth Summit in Rio de Janeiro, in the formulation of the *Convention on Biological Diversity* (CBD) – the almost-universal blueprint for global conservation.

The language and rationale of the CBD was couched firmly in terms of the economic and social benefits that efforts to save genes, species and ecosystems would bring. This appealed to technocrats and led to considerable increases in government funds to support biodiversity and multi-million dollar projects to integrate conservation and development in and around national parks in developing countries.

On the tenth anniversary of the Earth Summit, governments committed to 'a more effective and coherent implementation of the Convention and to achieve, by 2010, a significant reduction of the current rate of biodiversity loss'. Sadly, the 2010 report is expected to communicate disappointing progress on the seven focal areas that make up the overall target. Optimists argue that this will sting governments into more serious action. Others ask whether the very notion of biodiversity is a spent force. Government funding for international biodiversity is declining, partly because conservationists have struggled to prove their arguments that losing species has significant negative economic and social consequences and

THE RISE OF BIODIVERSITY (*cont.*)

partly because other causes (for example, wars, poverty and climate change) have placed new demands on finite budgets. It also seems that the technical term 'biodiversity' might be a turn-off for many. People are arguably more motivated by a combination of feelings, imagination, beliefs and rationality. Unfortunately, in the language of biodiversity older moral and aesthetic arguments for conservation barely get a look in.

A wide variety of national groups signed up to the BirdLife coalition, from large and well-established bird conservation organisations such as the RSPB (UK), Vogelbescherming (the Netherlands) and the Wild Bird Society of Japan, to smaller organisations, some little more than bird-watching clubs, such as the Bird Conservation Society of Nepal. The partnership also included organisations with a wider conservation remit, such as the Bombay Natural History Society of India and the Harabon Foundation in the Philippines that sought an international presence. Almost overnight, BirdLife was established as a major force in international conservation, laying claim to impressive geographical coverage and membership. Together, BirdLife and WWF were conservation's first organisations with an international membership. Other major international conservation organisations, notably the Wildlife Conservation Society and the Nature Conservancy and Conservation International in the USA and Fauna and Flora International in the UK, have evolved organisational structures similar to transnational corporations. They are internationally orientated but nationally based organisations, whose head offices manage a network of regional offices and national sub-offices staffed by internationally trained and recruited professionals, whose mix of nationalities and ethnicities reflects that of the country in which they are located.

Branded conservation: the rise of Conservation International

In the world of conservation policy, science and finance, Conservation International is probably the best-known – and arguably the most influential – conservation organisation. It is the newest of the big players, formed between 1987 and 1989 by breakaway groups from Nature Conservancy and WWF-US. Under the dynamic and charismatic leadership of Peter Seligmann and Russell Mittermier, Conservation International attracted some of America's new breed of entrepreneurs on to its board (notably the Intel founder and multi-millionaire Gordon Moore): all people who really understood the power of branding.

By the 1990s, numerous conservation groups jostled for the attention of decision-makers and donors. The competition intensified after the 1992 Earth Summit, with the promise of massive new intergovernmental funds for biodiversity conservation. Conservation International realised that hard-pressed bureaucrats would suddenly have the responsibility for dispersing these funds. It viewed them as customers in need of a service: the service they provided was an efficient and scientifically robust conservation scheme targeted at these new funds.

Conservation International revamped an idea – 'biodiversity hotspots' – originally outlined by the independent Oxford-based scientist, Norman Myers. Myers argued that global conservation efforts should be focused into the eighteen regions of the world that supported the greatest species diversity most under threat of destruction. Taking inspiration from the corporate sector, Conservation International focused investment not so much on the areas under threat as on the 'hotspots' brand. They engaged leading public relations companies, published a cover story in and supplement to the prestigious science journal *Nature* and hosted high-level conferences, seminars and presentations in 'hotspot countries'. These and other measures successfully established biodiversity hotspots as the first branded conservation solution.

From the perspective of organisational development, this is one of conservation's most successful strategies. 'Hotspots' had the key qualities of a great brand: it made people aware of the biodiversity conservation solution (strategic awareness), had scientific approval and credibility (perceived quality) and, at the time, was the only global scheme on offer (singular distinction). In the three years following the launch of the hotspots initiative, US$750 million of biodiversity funds were channelled through Conservation International, enabling it to extend its organisational reach across the world and across sectors. 'Conservation' and 'biodiversity hotspots' became almost synonymous. Conservation International became a magnet for wealthy and influential people seeking to associate themselves with the conservation agenda, conservation's first 'green-chip' organisation and the preferred partner for the world's blue-chip companies and celebrities who wanted to align themselves with efforts to conserve the world's remaining habitats and species.

The modern organisational landscape

We have emphasised the origins and diversity of internationally focused conservation organisations and barely touched on the many – perhaps the majority – of smaller organisations that concentrate on a particular issue, region or species and continue a proud tradition of natural history and site preservation. Several of these are internationally known, with a long and distinguished history, such as the Sierra Club, founded in 1892 by John Muir and others to protect wilderness and promote enjoyment and appreciation of America's wild places. Others are well known locally, such as EcoTrust, which focuses on the conservation of the rainforest of the Pacific North West and promotes the wonderful idea of the 'Salmon Nation', whose citizens choose to live in a place in which economic, ecological and social conditions are improving. Other examples include the UK Bat Conservation Society (www.bats.org.uk), the Malayan Natural History Society (Malaysia) and the Tobagan Buccoo Reef Trust (www.buccooreef.org).

It may indeed be impossible to calculate how many conservation organisations there are around the world. The greatest proliferation of NGOs is in developing countries and while many of these have conservation and environment programmes, they tend to be part of a wide portfolio of activities that typically include poverty, empowerment and other social issues. Such statistics could be meaningless: increasingly, conservation organisations work in partnership and with organisations from other sectors. What might matter most in the future is the strength, composition, reach and numbers either of conservation networks or of networks in which conservation has a compelling and authoritative voice.

3
Building influence

Conservation's broad aim is to save species, habitats and ecosystems from destruction. But achieving it is fraught with difficulty: enormous cultural, economical and political pressures – from uncontrolled population growth, rural poverty and the expansion of agriculture to hunting and the illegal trade in wildlife – are ranged against it. To achieve their goals, conservationists need to increase their influence over governments and markets, take direct action when necessary and build public support. A range of strategies and methods has been developed to establish conservation as a force within the complex structures of governments, corporations, communities and individuals. These influence-building activities are the topic of this chapter.

Since the 1970s, there have been fundamental changes in the processes that create change in societies. States have increasingly ceded power upwards, either to supra-national political entities, such as the European Union and intergovernmental bodies such as the World Trade Organization, or devolved power downwards to local government. Once-powerful ministries no longer directly implement their policies; instead, they sub-contract the delivery of public services to private companies and charities.

Such changes reflect the ascendancy of the neo-liberal belief that free markets can deliver goods to the public more effectively than governments. Consequently, more institutions and individuals are involved in setting and delivering policy. From a conservation perspective, key decisions are now made at many different levels, from international organisations to local communities. In some ways, this is good for conservation;

giving it many more opportunities and avenues for influence. In others, it is not: the amorphous nature of modern governance means there is no single or collective entity to make decisions or determine outcomes. Conservation uses five main approaches to influence government and commerce:

Relationship-building – developing relationships with conservation-minded officials, bureaucrats and employees of corporations who may see benefits in joining with a conservation cause.

Expert advice – generating and communicating expert and original advice and analysis about the state of the natural world, what threatens it, and possible solutions.

Creating standards – writing assessment, categorisation and measurement standards to turn agreements, laws and commitments into tangible, evaluable practices.

Framing issues – shaping how conservation issues are thought about (framed) and promoting public and media interest in the best solutions and actions.

Direct action – acquiring and managing land and captive populations of critically endangered species.

This is not an exhaustive list; for example, it does not include taking governments to court if they fail to enforce conservation-related law. This approach is used often in the US but rarely elsewhere. Nor does it include the raising and spending of money, which underpins everything else in the list. Financing conservation is fundamentally important: we will cover this in Chapter 6.

Change is now enacted through networks; conservation must operate across a broad front, blending traditional approaches and new tactics. The traditional target is to influence governments and intergovernment organisations to pass laws, negotiate international agreements, enact policies and commission research, form partnerships and allocate the necessary budget, personnel, land and other resources to ensure the implementation of conservation-related policy and law. However, more recently conservation has been experimenting with new tactics involving the creation of market 'pulls and pushes', for example attempting to influence the purchasing and investment decisions of consumers, companies and institutions such as pension funds, and the practices of resource-based industries.

The two most popular (and obvious) tactical approaches are advocacy and campaigning. Advocacy is the art of access, of being persuasive yet reasonable. It is about being invited to participate in important decision-making forums, being listened to and respected and sustaining long-term access to the corridors of power. Policy advocacy is the bread and butter of many large conservation organisations. In contrast, campaigning is about increasing the cost of inaction. For governments, it might be the political cost of being pilloried in the media, fending off difficult questions from opposition politicians or the effort of answering a mountain of critical letters. For corporations, it might be the cost of consumer boycotts, loss of licences, finding it more difficult to hold on to employees or the tarnishing of the vitally important but wonderfully intangible 'brand value'.

A more subtle strategy is to shape the way people think about their relationship with the natural world. Everyone – experts and public alike – makes sense of the complexities of the world by mentally grouping miscellaneous facts, metaphors, images and values into a 'frame'; a mental noticeboard on which new leaflets, photos, memos and posters are constantly added over the top of older information. The frame determines what gets talked about and in what way. Effective communication on conservation is about creating, maintaining and transforming its frames. Framing conservation for the public is closely linked to advocacy and campaigning; together, these strategies form a suite of awareness-raising activities that combine to embed conservation in the collective psyche.

Framing conservation

Moving conservation from being a specialist to a public concern and ultimately transforming it into a cultural force means aligning its agendas with issues that are important and meaningful to people: things like cultural and national identity, health and well-being, self-realisation, adventure and compassion and concern for others. The eminent American ecologist and conservationist, E.O. Wilson, uses the word 'biophilia' to refer to the innate human affiliation with the natural world and living systems. This means conservationists often push against an open door when it comes to engaging people – the news, entertainment and educational media, the tourism industry and other cultural activities are quick to link themselves with conservation.

A great campaign creates cultural ripples that shape longer-term and deeper understandings about the relationships between society and nature. Environmental organisations – in particular Greenpeace – have arguably been more effective than conservation organisations in aligning their causes with popular culture. The image of Greenpeace's small inflatable boats taking on Russian whalers in 1970 is a classic example. This version of the deeply culturally embedded 'David and Goliath' story aligned Greenpeace's campaign to 'Save the Whale' with two huge contemporary themes – the Cold War and people-power. Climate change is the latest – and arguably most serious – concept to unite the conservation and environmental movements. Before the early 2000s, the climate change debate was packed with scientific facts and projections but struggled to penetrate the public's concern and interest. But a poignant image of a forlorn polar bear swimming in an ocean without icebergs endowed climate change with a cultural and sentimental significance that resonated with the broader public consciousness.

Recently, conservation may have struggled to find a big issue or idea but conservationists have not lost their talent for keeping an appreciation of nature and concern for its survival in the mainstream of popular culture. Two examples from 2008, one from each side of the Atlantic, illustrate current innovative work. Conservation International linked rainforest deforestation with American celebrity culture by convincing Hollywood 'A-lister' Harrison Ford to have a patch of his chest hairs waxed (ripped off) on camera. During his ordeal, Ford turned to the camera and declared 'every acre lost there [the rainforest of some developing world country], hurts here [in the developed world]!' Meanwhile, WWF Portugal teamed up with the soccer club Benfica (Sporting Lisbon) to generate public support for their campaign to save the Portuguese white-tailed eagle and, more generally, bring conservation into the life of Lisbon's football-obsessed population. An eagle, Victory, sits atop the Benfica emblem. Newspapers and television channels spread a (spoof) story that Victory was missing. Players and other VIPs appealed for the eagle's safe return and the club organised a 'day of the eagle'. At the next home game, Victory was missing from the stadium, including from the emblems on the player's shirts. Supporters were given feather-shaped leaflets and asked to wave them as they called for the return of the eagle. Their calls were answered as a magnificent eagle circled down into the stadium and alighted on top of the emblem. This original and emotive strategy united Benfica fans in saying 'the wild eagle is our eagle and our lives will be diminished without it'.

Both these events aligned conservation with cultural icons – a celebrity and a football team – and reached out to new and younger audiences by posting short videos on YouTube. Both were newsworthy, and raised the public profile of conservation. Moreover, in Portugal, WWF subtly presented conservation as part of a people's cultural identity.

Creating effective regulatory frameworks

Clever media campaigns, particularly at the local level, are vital for keeping conservation on the political agenda and ensuring politicians and bureaucrats stay receptive to conservationists' advocacy and lobbying. Nationally, and especially internationally, most conservation policy is conceived and framed by scientists and policy experts working with senior bureaucrats and advisors. Conservation organisations exert their influence by becoming part of these policy communities. Individual conservationists working as government employees, academics and consultants are naturally part of the structures that create policy and legal frameworks.

The places where conservation-related decisions are made are many and varied. They range from big international events, such as the 2007 Conference on Climate Change, held in Bali, to the numerous small working groups which discuss and prepare particular policies or draft legislation. Some are conservation-specific, such as the Convention on International Trade in Endangered Species, while others are more generic, such as the many committees associated with the European Union's Common Agricultural Policy whose goal is to ensure that conservation stays 'in the frame'. Effective advocacy means identifying the key policy networks and committees, getting on to those committees, and exerting an influence either on the way the decisions are made or the decisions themselves. Conservationists strive for a systematic, ordered and authoritative implementation of conservation policy nationally and internationally. One effective strategy is to work closely with intergovernmental organisations to initiate and influence international conventions that countries feel obliged to translate into national laws and regulations.

The trade in wildlife was the subject of the first modern international conservation convention, the Convention on

International Trade in Endangered Species (CITES). The IUCN started the process, preparing and circulating a draft to 90 governments and international organisations. The US Department of the Interior was unimpressed by this first draft, so the Audubon Society (a US-based bird conservation charity) sent its experts to work with the newly formed United Nations Environment Programme (UNEP) on a revision that would satisfy the Americans. This revision formed the basis of international negotiations at a conference, held in Washington in 1973, which resulted in CITES.

Table 2 CITES appendices

Appendix	Description
Appendix 1	Species that are threatened with extinction. Trade in specimens of these species is permitted only in exceptional circumstances.
Appendix 2	Species not necessarily threatened with extinction, but in which trade must be controlled in order to avoid utilisation incompatible with their survival.
	[*This is the most political category, because it provides a forum for interest groups to lobby for increased protection and raises questions of how and by whom assessments of 'incompatibility' (termed non-detrimental findings) should be made.*]
Appendix 3	Species that are protected in at least one country, which has asked certain other countries for assistance in controlling the trade.

CITES enshrines some of the fundamental themes of conservation – the wise use of natural resources, the ending of the unnecessary slaughter of wildlife and avoiding extinctions – identified by Roosevelt nearly a century earlier (see Chapter 2). CITES legislates the belief that human use of and trade in wildlife should not endanger wild populations. It has attracted near-universal support: 173 countries are signatories to CITES and, since its ratification, only one species (Spix's macaw) is known to have become extinct primarily as a result of trading. CITES is an example of the 'laws and fines' regulatory approach to conservation. It obliges signatory nations to establish regulations based on a package of species lists, catch quotas, permits and fines and reporting, supported by national legislation. Rare species, those vulnerable to over-harvesting and their products are placed on one of three CITES appendices (see Table 2) according to their perceived level of endangerment and national conservation priorities. CITES is the reason that tourists can't buy ebony sculptures in Kenya or bring an ivory carving back from safari in South Africa.

The importance of a close relationship between conservation organisations and government is illustrated by another piece of landmark conservation legislation, the European Birds Directive. In the late 1970s, the chairman of the International Council for Bird Preservation's (ICBP) Continental Section happened to be a lawyer within the European Commission (the EU's executive arm). He secured the support of a commissioner for a directive on wild birds, developed in consultation with the ICBP. This Directive, on the Conservation of Wild Birds, better known as the Birds Directive, came into being in 1979 and has had a lasting impact. Not only did it impose tight controls on hunting, killing and trading in wild birds but also required EC countries to designate areas (known as Special Protection Areas, SPAs) for the protection of rare and endangered species. SPAs, and Special Areas of Conservation (designated under the 1992 Habitats Directive), are the backbone of nature conservation in Europe and together contribute substantially to the EU's network of protected areas, termed Natura 2000.

The mere signing of a convention or passing of a law is not, unfortunately, enough to bring about change. To achieve widespread and uniform implementation of legal frameworks conservation organisations need to support (or take responsibility for) three key activities: the creation of categorisation and assessment schemes, the publication of detailed implementation guidelines and the improvement of scientific and technical capacity in countries where these are lacking. Conservationists are arguably achieving their greatest impact through the invention and establishment of categorisation and assessment schemes. These schemes simplify nature and make it manageable, reducing its complexity into quantifiable, measureable forms that can be assessed and legislated.

The CITES Red Data Book system classifies species into 'critically endangered', 'endangered', 'vulnerable' and 'least risk', using scientifically robust criteria. This system gives the three appendices described in Table 2 meaning and, crucially, provides for monitoring of how well countries are complying with the convention. In the Birds Directive, the EC wanted to monitor whether member countries were fulfilling their conservation obligations. They asked the ICBP secretariat in Cambridge to prepare an EU-wide inventory of 'Important Bird Areas' (IBAs). The ICBP cleverly converted the Directive's list of four types of species needing protection (Article 4) into a set of quantifiable site-selection criteria and took the bold step of making both the criteria and site inventory public. Their book, *Important Bird Areas of Europe*, published in 1989, allowed citizens to hold their governments to account for their conservation actions. Moreover, Eastern European countries wishing to join the EU were required to identify Special Protection Areas as a condition of accession. The BirdLife European network, which had become the authority on systematic identification of sites, supported bird conservation groups in accession countries in preparing IBA inventories for their governments. This helped build new relationships between conservationists and government officials in post-Communist countries, as well as ensuring that key sites got the recognition and protection they needed. Conservation International is currently extending and applying the IBA criteria to other species groups to identify Key Biodiversity Areas (KBAs). This provides a bigger-scale target for conservation investments in biodiversity hotspots and allows the monitoring of compliance with the Convention on Biological Diversity and progress towards biodiversity-related targets of other major international environmental initiatives, such as the Millennium Ecosystem Assessment.

THE CBD: CONSERVATION'S UNIVERSAL FRAMEWORK

The main legislative response of the international community to the perceived conservation crisis is the Convention on Biological Diversity (CBD), a remarkable international agreement, negotiated during the Earth Summit in Rio de Janeiro in 1992. The CBD has three main aims: the conservation of biodiversity, the sustainable use of its components and the sharing of benefits from commercial and other use of genetic resources in a fair and equitable way. The CBD is pragmatic, with a clear focus on sustainably using natural resources.

Governments have to respond to the CBD by outlining strategies, plans and programmes for national conservation. Many countries have developed national biodiversity strategies or biodiversity action plans (identifying practical steps) as a way of fulfilling their obligations. However, implementation means parties must engage in complicated and uncertain legal and political processes. Because translation of the CBD into national legislation is so complex, many countries (for example, the USA) found the commitments did not mesh sufficiently with their domestic institutions and they refused to ratify the Convention.

The CBD has been criticised for having few measurable targets and deadlines. Moreover, the emphasis on the sovereign right of states over their own biological resources makes the management of biodiversity across national boundaries deeply problematic. But, despite its drawbacks and flaws, the CBD provides much of the legislative framework for global conservation and is one of the main pillars of global conservation.

Categorisation schemes tell governments *what* to conserve; information on *how* to conserve is typically given as practice guidelines. Writing and developing practice guidelines – the business of many conservation organisations – calls for careful technical writing, political manoeuvring and, above all, tenacity and is clearly *not* the most glamorous aspect of conservation action. However, because of the influence and reach of such guidelines, conservation groups have become very savvy in ensuring that they have a say in shaping their content. The influence and credibility of guidelines greatly depends on who issues them: the Animal Committee of CITES publishes guidelines on how a state should determine whether a trade is detrimental to a wild population. These have great authority, because they are issued by an official committee of an international convention.

Categorisation schemes and guidelines combine with a third component for establishing effective conservation institutions: capacity-building. 'Capacity-building' is something of a catch-all term, essentially meaning anything that improves the ability of a conservation group or organisation. Capacity-building may include writing manuals, running training workshops and courses or working with staff in partner organisations on field projects. Most donors now require conservation groups to demonstrate a strong capacity-building component in funding applications. Whatever the complexities of its delivery, the basic idea is simple: conservation conventions will be more effective if the relevant organisations in a country possess the expertise and skills necessary to implement them.

Non-state conservation governance

The creation of regulatory regimes and their supporting institutions has been the key means through which conservation has exerted its influence, especially internationally. However, this approach has a number of inherent weaknesses, such as the assumption that governments possess the authority, will and capacity to enforce regulations. Sadly, this is not always the case in many developing countries, where conservation action is often most urgently required. A second weakness is the inflexibility and bluntness of many regulatory instruments: for example, if a new and collectable species is discovered, CITES cannot offer it any legal protection until it has been formally named and listed in an appendix. This can take several years, during which collection could render the new species extinct. A third weakness is that the increasing complexity of international relations makes it very time-consuming to get conservation issues on to international agendas; some high-priority issues may never make it. The failure of the 1992 Earth Summit to secure support for an international convention to regulate the huge demand for tropical hardwoods gave conservation organisations the impetus to try a different approach: an attempt to govern the conservation of hardwoods without involving governments by using the influencing strategies (outlined at the beginning of this chapter) to modify the supply chain for timber.

This idea was inspired by the successes of consumer movements, which had changed the performance, price and quality of products and services by enabling people to make informed choices about purchases. The development and dissemination of comparison tools, such as the *Which Guides* (www.which.co.uk) were central to the influence of consumer groups. Conservation and environmental organisations wanted to harness purchasers' power and create change throughout the supply chains of natural products to improve environmental (and social) sustainability. They achieved this by devising categorisation schemes, developing verifiable standards and criteria (now called certification) and creating governance systems that established their credibility and authority. Certification is rapidly becoming a major tool of conservation practice. WWF, and the

US-based Rainforest Alliance, were its pioneers but many other organisations are now engaging with this form of market-based conservation. The Marine Stewardship Council's certification system is gaining popular support as a way for consumers to feel confident that the fish they eat are from sustainable stocks. The Forest Stewardship Council (FSC) is another model scheme (see Figure 6). The FSC was initiated in 1992 by a group of concerned businesses and conservation NGOs that created a new organisation with a novel structure. The heart of the FSC is certification: a set of principles, criteria and categories that give consumers a guarantee of the sustainability and traceability of harvested timber. Forestry operations, traders and retailers in the supply chain are assessed by accredited independent certifiers, who are regularly audited by the FSC. These certifiers issue two types of certificate: a 'forest management unit' certificate and a 'chain of custody' certificate, which both permit the producer or retailer to display the FSC logo (Figure 7). The companies pay the fees of the certifying agency.

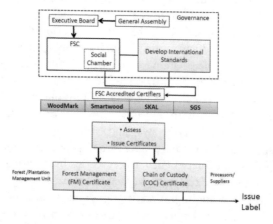

Figure 6 The structure of the Forest Stewardship Council (FSC)

Figure 7 The FSC logo – now seen on wood products from around the world

Part of the appeal of certification is that it offers a rapid response to policy issues and is a way to bypass the bureaucracy, inertia and politics of international government. In a bid to reduce dependency on fossil fuels and bolster green credentials, the European Union and the USA recently legislated that a percentage of fuel should be derived from biofuels. These fuels are produced from crops such as oil palm and soya, mainly grown in the tropics. The conservation movement is trying to deal with this ill-conceived policy, which, quite apart from its consequences on global food prices, has promoted rapid expansion of oil palm agriculture and quickened clearance of the last remnants of lowland rainforest in Sumatra and elsewhere. Campaigns against legislation linked to energy security were unlikely to succeed, so WWF initiated round-table talks, inviting leading plantation companies and manufacturers of products containing palm oil. Members of the Round Table on Sustainable Palm Oil (RSPO) have agreed practices that will reduce the conservation and social impacts of palm oil plantation. Key to the voluntary co-operation of companies is a special scheme developed by the FSC, the High Conservation Value Forest (HCVF) scheme, which identifies forests vital to conservation that lie within a company's plantation concession.

The RSPO illustrates how voluntary, market-based approaches have moved beyond using the power of informed consumers to including corporate brands and corporate social responsibility. Many leading companies recognise the value of a good public image in securing access to markets, securing cheaper investment and attracting the best staff. They are attracted by the idea of voluntarily operating beyond government-set regulations. When companies are not willing actively to follow conservation policies, conservation organisations have a number of strategies they can try. Conservationists, and their colleagues in the environmental movement, are becoming adept both at dangling carrots and waving sticks before companies sensitive to public opinion. They map the networks of exchange and commerce that link companies and natural resources and identify who is particularly open to influence and from whom.

In contrast to the formal policy communities described earlier, influence in this field is built through loose policy networks, many of which operate in the hidden crevices of the offices, cafés and email networks inhabited by conservation activists. The Indonesian–owned company APRIL operates a huge pulp mill in Sumatra, fed both from acacia plantations (converted from rainforest) and by truckloads of timber that arrive with 'no questions asked'. Paper pulp, like palm oil, is a difficult target for ethical consumerism, because it is sold whole-sale and incorporated into a range of products. This made it difficult to identify any single company to be the focus of concerted public campaigns. In 1997, Friends of the Earth (FoE) groups in Finland and the UK, and a group of smaller, more radical, environmental and indigenous rights groups started targeting wholesalers of APRIL pulp products and campaigning for a boycott. Pulp mills require huge investment; cleverly, the groups analysed the finances of the pulp and paper sector and found that APRIL owed large sums of money to eight leading financial institutions. FoE published a report: *Paper Dragons, Hidden Tigers*, which exposed the role of these banks in defor-estation and demanded they uphold the principles of ethical investment, such as the Equator Principles (www.equator-principles.com), to which several were already signatories. The banks' response was to take active measures to avoid becoming the target of a serious NGO campaign.

WWF adopted a more collaborative approach and was conveniently on hand to offer APRIL some solutions. The first was to adopt the FSC's HCVF standard and apply it to identify and protect key forest patches within APRIL's concessions. The second was to improve and tighten timber procurement and ensure the mill did not buy timber from illegal logging. In return, WWF agreed not to join a boycott campaign. APRIL agreed that a 100,000 hectare block of forest, *Teso Nilo*, could be proposed as a new national park. Interestingly the company went further, conducting its own analysis of ethical markets and

SELLING A SPECIES TO SAVE IT

An initiative of the British Cactus and Succulent Society exemplifies the extent to which market-based thinking, and a more inclusive model of engagement, are taking root in modern conservation. When a new and very geographically restricted cactus species, *Yavia cryptocarpa*, was discovered in Argentina in 2001, the society quickly realised that it could rapidly be collected to extinction. They asked the team who discovered it to delay its announcement until the plant had been successfully propagated. Once a good breeding stock had been established, the exciting new discovery was announced, together with the message that seeds were available for purchase.

The massive threat to wild orchid populations has been similarly addressed by the development of propagation techniques and mass production methods on farms in Florida and Holland. Becoming part of the specialist networks of trade and exchange is providing opportunities for individuals and specialist groups to become active and more effective conservationists.

corporate social responsibility. APRIL has subsequently become a member of the World Business Council on Sustainable Development. This illustrates how environmental groups can use their skills in policy advocacy, campaigning and developing categorisation schemes to influence the behaviour of major corporations and supply chains. It also exemplifies the complex tactics by which more confrontational environmental NGOs kick open the door of corporate indifference, through which more conciliatory conservation organisations can enter. Indeed, a distinguishing characteristic of many conservation organisations is their willingness to work with corporations (or governments) that show a genuine commitment to changing their destructive ways. As we will see in Chapter 7, these relationships are not beyond criticism.

Some of the larger American NGOs, notably the Nature Conservancy and Conservation International, have taken the market-based approach a step further by recruiting gifted economists who have developed financial tools to harness the power of capital and markets in the cause of conservation. Many of these tools are designed to generate new sources of funding, as well as provide financial incentives to protect habitats and sites. Notable examples are the transfer of land-use rights towards conservation (known as conservation easements), debt-for-nature swaps and a new mechanism for protecting forests, Reduced Emissions from Deforestation and Degradation (REDD). These will be discussed in Chapter 6.

4
Science-based conservation

If we are to save species, habitats and ecosystems from destruction, we need to know fundamental facts about the natural world: how many species are there on Earth, what does 'rare' mean, how much habitat does a species need, what is a healthy ecosystem and what happens to a species when there are only a few individuals left? Only science can provide answers to these questions although, as we shall see, even it has its limits. Science is a tool, a systematic way of gathering information and understanding processes, not an end in itself. If conservationists, and conservation organisations, are to bring to life their vision of the human–nature relationship, they need to ask the right questions for science to answer.

Science is also vitally important in giving conservation organisations credibility and legitimacy in their interactions with other groups. 'Hard' science, based on strong empirical evidence, is almost a prerequisite if conservation is to be taken seriously by governments. Governments want to be seen to make rational decisions, without recourse to faith or opinion. Science offers the promise of rationality and guards conservation from charges of sentimentality or representing the values of the élite. And the ability to 'talk science' and back up theories with evidence, conveys considerable authority.

Conceptual foundations

Conservation science is, like the natural world it seeks to describe and understand, vast, complex and multi-layered.

Modern conservationists draw ideas from a range of scientific disciplines: for example, ecology, animal behaviour and genetics. One of conservation's great visionaries, Graham Caughley, pointed out that the majority of conservation research falls into one of two paradigms: studies that seek to understand the direct and immediate causes of population decline (the declining population paradigm) and those that address the negative consequences of existing in a small population (the small population paradigm). Unfortunately, as Caughley recognised, these two paradigms rarely intersect. Conservation science is trying to

THE ORIGINS OF CONSERVATION SCIENCE

Before the 1970s, conservation was largely a mix of forestry, agricultural and biological science. A more distinct 'science of conservation' started to take shape in the late 1970s and early 1980s, when conservation biology was recognised as a sub-discipline worthy of academic study in its own right, with dedicated journals, textbooks and university courses. Conceptually, conservation biology has drawn heavily on concepts and theories from ecology, population biology and natural resource management although it has always been interested in perspectives from the humanities and, especially and increasingly, from the social sciences.

The first international conference dedicated to conservation biology took place in 1978 at the University of California, San Diego. However, the study of conservation biology really took off with the founding of the US-based *Society for Conservation Biology* (SCB) in 1986 and the publication of the first edition of their influential journal, *Conservation Biology*, in 1987. Founded and supported by some of the giants of modern conservation and ecology – E.O. Wilson, Ernst Mayr, Michael Soule, Paul Erlich – the society has led conservation science into the twenty-first century and has been instrumental both in legitimising conservation as an academic discipline and providing the hard data and strong concepts on which modern conservation practice is founded.

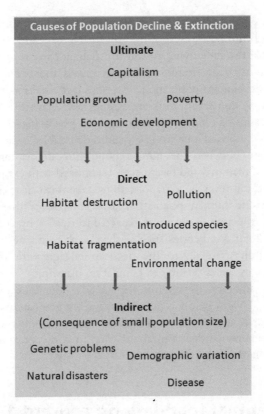

Figure 8 Extinction drivers

develop ideas and approaches that will allow the accurate identification of species and populations that are most at risk of extinction.

The biggest problem conservation scientists face in developing a truly predictive science is that species population decline and extinction are complex, linked and hierarchical problems (see Figure 8). Habitat loss has been identified as the key driver of population decline but is not usually the reason a species becomes extinct. The last few individuals of a species often meet their end through disease, or are unable to find a mate. Moreover, the underlying reasons for habitat loss are normally associated with economic development and the needs of an expanding human population. To discover the reasons for habitat loss, conservationists are taking their science into the distant realms of economics, sociology and psychology. A study from 2004, carried out in 114 countries, established a strong relationship between the human population density and the number of mammal and bird species threatened with extinction. If this relationship is extrapolated to take into account the rapidly rising human population, the number of threatened species in the average nation is expected to rise 7% by 2020 and 14% by 2050. Predictions such as these alert teams developing conservation strategies to the need to engage with broader public policy issues relating to population planning.

Contemporary conservation science now contains some core concepts. The list below is not exhaustive but gives an overview of the ideas and tools that influence conservationists as they make fundamental decisions about what to conserve, where to conserve and how to conserve.

Conceptual foundations: concept 1, species–area relationship

There is convincing evidence, from long-standing observation, of a strong relationship between the size of a habitat and the number of species within it: the species–area relationship. This simple concept is important because habitat destruction is the chief threat to populations and species, and so central to the prediction of extinction rate. The loss of natural habitats has almost ceased in Europe and North America, but continues and is severe in most parts of the tropics. Unfortunately, the tropics contain the most species-rich habitats and the places where our knowledge about biodiversity is least complete.

The species–area relationship is used to estimate how many species might be lost when a habitat is reduced. In Singapore, where less than one per cent of the original forest cover remains, habitat loss is estimated to have caused the extinction of 34% to 87% of the butterflies, fish, birds and mammals that once lived on the island. Theoretical models of the relationship between species numbers and area, developed from studies of oceanic islands, predict that a 95% reduction in the area of a habitat will cause the loss of half of the species that live within it.

The species–area relationship can also be used to predict extinction at a very large scale. E.O. Wilson predicted in 1992 that deforestation may commit as many as 27,000 species to extinction each year. We say 'committed to extinction' because habitat destruction is rarely the direct cause of extinction. A habitat which has been considerably reduced in size takes many years to relax back to the point where there is equilibrium between new species arriving and existing species becoming extinct. The profoundly disturbing implication is that we may not yet have seen the real consequences of the recent global spate of habitat destruction. Many habitats hold an 'extinction debt', waiting to be paid. More positively, conservationists have a brief opportunity to save 'alive but ultimately doomed' species from extinction.

Conservation International has taken the logic of the species-area relationship a step further, creating a constantly ticking 'extinction clock' (find via www.conservation.org). The clock was set by combining extinction estimates based on habitat destruction with the latest models of the impact of climate change on biodiversity. Their mean estimate for the time between 2000 and 2050 is that 25% of five million species will become extinct: that is, 1.3 million species, or roughly one species becoming extinct every 20 minutes. Such figures are alarming (26,000 species have gone 'extinct' while we were writing this book!) but they grab the attention of high-level policy-makers, provide a powerful argument for forest protection and raise public awareness of conservation issues. Extinction is something of a 'hot potato'; high numbers strike an alarm and are reported in the media but extinction can be classified and assessed in many ways – no estimate of future extinction rates can be absolutely accurate.

Conceptual foundations: concept 2, habitat matrix

Habitat loss does not just mean reduction in area – habitats are also lost through fragmentation. The degree to which a habitat is fragmented can be measured but the effects on wild populations are far less easy to predict. Fragmentation has at least four different effects on a habitat (and thus potential consequences for species and populations): a reduction in the amount of habitat available, an increase in the number of habitat patches, a decrease in the size of patches and an increase in the isolation of patches.

Conceptually, it is very important to distinguish the ways in which changes in habitat pattern might influence the wildlife of an area. Habitat loss has a strong and consistently negative effect on species diversity; breaking a habitat up into fragments, with little loss of actual area, has a much weaker – and sometimes even positive – impact on species numbers. Habitat loss and fragmentation affect different species in different ways. 'Generalist' species, able to use both the edges and the interior of a habitat fragment, will be only be affected by habitat loss. But species that are restricted to the interior of a habitat, such as many forest birds and mammals, will suffer greater population decline through fragmentation than would be predicted from habitat loss alone. Species that live on the edges of habitats (ecotones) might even increase in number if fragmentation brings an increase in the absolute amount of habitat available. Clearly, it is not just the extent of habitat loss but also the pattern of the remaining habitats and the types of species present that influence the model and tempo of species loss and population decline.

Forest fragments have been described as 'islands' because more recent studies flag the importance of considering the kind of habitat that surrounds an isolated forest fragment. A more realistic view might be to think of habitat fragments as patches of 'quality' habitat embedded in a 'matrix' of other, more or less hospitable, habitats. Hospitability depends very much on the ecology of the species in question: grassland surrounding forest patches may be a barrier to amphibians' movement but not to that of many birds. Habitat patches in human-dominated landscapes may be islands for some species but not others. Conservation science and management is consequently turning towards managing whole landscapes, rather than just protected areas and the habitat fragments embedded within them. This may involve connecting reserves and patches via habitat corridors or influencing the management of land use to maintain or improve 'permeability'.

Continuing habitat loss in many ecosystems is inevitable, so the key question for conservationists is not how to prevent further habitat loss but rather, how much habitat is enough? The traditional scientific approach is to develop models that can predict the area required to sustain an endangered population for a substantial period (centuries rather than decades). This is a prudent, testable, approach but current levels of international support for conservation mean that other, distinctly non-scientific, criteria can be used to determine the size and shape of protected areas, with little reference to whether or not they are large enough for the conservation of the species for which they are 'designed'.

Conceptual foundations: concept 3, metapopulation

One of the most obvious ecological consequences of fragmentation is that large coherent populations are broken into many small populations. These sub-populations may be completely isolated but, more often than not, remain loosely connected through a greater or lesser degree of species' movement. These fragmented (but biologically connected) populations are called 'metapopulations'; conservation scientists have developed a range of techniques to study how such populations behave and what the consequences of metapopulations are for species management and conservation.

Conservation management strategies and interventions can be designed that benefit either each sub-population or the whole metapopulation. Interestingly, these strategies are often very different. A study on a sub-population of a small shrub growing on the shaded floor of the eucalyptus forest of Australia suggested that the best conservation strategy was to reduce predation by rodents. However, the best conservation strategy to maintain the health of the metapopulation was to manage the risk of fire. Locally, rodents can be a problem but they do not affect all sub-populations to the same extent. Put another way, sub-populations driven to extinction by over-enthusiastic rodents will eventually be recolonised from elsewhere, whereas fire could sweep through the entire landscape and so threaten the existence of all the sub-populations. Generally, conserving a healthy metapopulation tends to focus on reserve design, building reserve networks, reintroductions and translocations and the creation of dispersal corridors.

Conceptual foundations: concept 4, ecosystems and the flux of nature

Species and populations are not, of course, discrete entities that react in simple, predictable ways to the structure and extent of their habitat. Species exist within complex food webs, whose structure can change dramatically, and often unpredictably, in response to the introduction of a new species, the loss or decline of a major predator or a shift in the local climate. Ecological communities are naturally in constant flux; the primary question for conservationists is not whether to allow change but how much and what sort of change.

This view of nature is quite different from the fragile, delicately balanced natural habitats frequently described in newspapers, magazines and books. The scientific view is that most ecosystems are constantly changing and, to an extent, resilient. However, sometimes a catastrophic event causes an ecosystem to shift from a diverse, species-rich community to a much simpler, less interesting assemblage of plants and animals. These phase shifts from high to low diversity are happening with increasing frequency in coral reefs around the world, due to a combination of pollution, over-fishing, rising sea temperatures and the loss of species that play important roles in maintaining the ecosystem. The exact causes of phase shifts are often difficult to identify but their consequences are obvious: reefs once teeming with brightly coloured fish become wastelands of coral rubble overgrown with algae, and support a tiny fraction of the species that once lived there.

Introduced species may also cause phase shifts. Species have always colonised new habitats and even, very occasionally, new continents but loose global trade barriers and cheap travel mean the volume and diversity of organisms being moved, both intentionally and unintentionally, has rocketed. These unwelcome, 'exotic', 'alien' or 'invasive' visitors are often cited as a major cause of loss of biodiversity, population decline and the transformation of habitats. Interestingly, recent scientific studies have cast doubt on whether many incoming species directly cause loss of biodiversity or merely take advantage of the empty space in habitats damaged by other means. This is supported by the

Figure 9 A 'medium-sized' Nile perch (photo © Mike Ladle)

observation that, in many habitats, there is a positive relationship between the numbers of non-native and native species – known in scientific circles as the 'invasion paradox'.

Paradox or not, there are many unambiguous examples of invasions leading to widespread extinctions and transformations of habitats. Islands (including those on inland lakes) appear to have suffered the most serious consequences of invasion. Perhaps the best- known example is the result of the introduction of the enormous predatory fish, the Nile perch, into Lake Victoria in East Africa. The introduction caused an enormous phase shift in the lake and is thought to be directly responsible for the extinction of more than two hundred species of cichlid (small, often colourful, fish popular with aquarium owners); many of these species were found only in this lake. The combined impact of the decline and extinction of many geographically restricted rare species and the rapid expansion in the geographic range of a few species of 'excellent' invaders may result in a far more homogenous – dare we say boring – natural world for future generations to enjoy.

One of the latest – and most highly publicised – threats to habitats and species is accelerated climate change: the rapid increase in mean global temperature that the Earth is currently experiencing. The climate has always changed, and ecosystems have always transformed, so are we justified in asking what is so different this time? Unfortunately, there are several good reasons to think that human-induced climate change will have enormous consequences for conservation. First, the Earth's climate may simply be changing too quickly for habitats and species to adjust their physiology, behaviour or location. This is especially true for species that migrate slowly, such as certain trees, mammals and invertebrates. Second, the massive habitat destruction and fragmentation that began in the late twentieth century means that most ecosystems are far less continuous and widespread than they were even in the early 1900s. Species once able to move to new and more appropriate habitats may find that there are simply no alternative habitats to go to. Lest we be accused of doom-mongering, it is worth noting that the effects of climate change are not yet fully apparent; there is little current evidence to implicate climate change in species extinction. The beautiful golden toad once found in the mountains of Costa Rica was thought to be such a victim but recent studies suggest that its extinction might be due to absorption of pesticides picked up by winds blowing over surrounding banana plantations.

In the absence of direct evidence, most attempts to quantify and understand the potential impacts of climate change on species and habitats have relied on the use of sophisticated computer simulations. These 'bioclimatic envelope models' are used to quantify the relationship between the current distribution of a species and the local climate. Perhaps the best publicised of these simulations was created by Professor Chris Thomas (then at the University of York) and his colleagues.

They used it to forecast the probability of extinction for species in an area representing about 20% of the Earth's land surface. The model predicted that 15% to 37% of species in the sample regions would be 'committed to extinction' by climate change between 2004 and 2050.

Given that it is now extremely unlikely that climate change will be stopped, let alone reversed, in the short term, many conservation scientists are beginning to accept the inevitability of substantial ecosystem change. There will be climate change winners and losers – a major role for conservation scientists is to identify which species will fall in which category as early as possible. Managing the effects of climate change on the natural world is one of the biggest challenges facing global conservation but it is a challenge with no easy solutions or quick answers.

Widespread and profound changes in the functioning of an ecosystem can be caused by the removal of 'keystone species'. A keystone species is a species that plays a critical role in maintaining the structure of an ecological community. Generally speaking, keystone species tend to be top-level predators or large herbivores – in other words, the sorts of species humans have traditionally hunted for meat, to protect their livestock or through fear for their personal safety. However, the advent of railways, roads and widely available guns, traps and nets has led to widespread over-hunting and over-harvesting, so that populations of keystone species have declined or disappeared altogether. Such unsustainable exploitation of wildlife and plants is often described as the second-biggest cause of recent extinctions (after habitat loss). The problem is especially acute in many developing countries, where the recent adoption of modern hunting techniques and technologies has sometimes led to massive increases in hunting efficiency. To be fair, this geographic trend is probably only apparent because the people of 'developed' countries hunted and collected a good proportion of indigenous species to extinction many centuries ago. Though it is difficult to believe, wolves, bears and beavers were once abundant in the British countryside.

Another high-profile, and related, problem is the taste that the people of many rainforest communities have for 'bushmeat' (meat from wild forest animals). Some cultures have a preference for such wild meat and, among certain social groups, serving meat from animals such as chimpanzees and bears at dinner parties or business dinners endows high status. More generally, the unsustainable hunting of mammals and birds in tropical forests has serious effects on other members of the forest community. The extent of these – currently hidden – consequences will largely be determined by the ability of non-game species to take on the ecological role of other, heavily exploited species – rather like putting on a substitute for an injured star player in a football team, we really have little idea how they will cope.

Bushmeat from tropical forests may grab newspaper headlines but the unsustainable exploitation of the oceans threatens the most significant impacts on a major ecosystem. For most global fisheries, the Food and Agriculture Organization's fisheries statistics clearly show a gradual transition from catches dominated by long-lived, predatory (fish-eating) species, from the top of the food chain, to catches predominantly made up of short-lived species 'grubbing around' at the bottom of the food chain eating plankton and invertebrates. This is called 'fishing down food webs'; a typical pattern is of increasing catches when stocks are high, followed by a rapid (and largely irreversible) transition to declining catches. The almost-complete loss of the Newfoundland cod fishery is just one example but the pattern is repeating around the world. Despite the obvious long-term consequences – and downright short-sightedness – of maintaining such unsustainable practices, little has so far been done to curb them, especially in the borderless (and often lawless) high seas fisheries. At the time of writing the prospects for immediate action continue to be almost unremittingly bleak.

Conceptual foundations: concept 5, small is not beautiful

Climate changes, pollution, unsustainable exploitation, invasive species or even habitat fragmentation do not cause the extinction of a species. The final culprit is almost always the tiny size of the last remaining populations. The final refuges of an endangered species are rarely completely destroyed. More often, the habitat suitable for a given species becomes so small in size that there are too few individuals to ensure the species' continued existence. But why can't a species survive almost indefinitely even at very low numbers? The answer lies in genetics, evolution and the unpredictable nature of the natural world.

When a population becomes very small it is largely thrown to the mercy of chance. Random factors – fluctuations in sex ratios or age distribution, the outbreak of disease or unusual weather events, may wipe out the last few individuals. Imagine a population of a very rare species that is down to its last three individuals – by sheer chance they could all be the same sex, two of them could be too old to breed, or they could all catch the same fatal disease. If a population stays small, sooner or later some essentially random event will wipe them out. Not only that but individuals in small populations inevitably end up breeding with close relatives. This causes the phenomenon of 'inbreeding depression', resulting in lower fertility and less viable offspring. Even if a group avoids inbreeding depression, the effects of genetic drift (a process by which certain gene variants may disappear from a population, thereby reducing genetic diversity) are greater in small populations. Genetic drift does not directly affect individuals; rather, it affects the ability of a population to evolutionarily adapt to new challenges such as outbreaks of disease or a changing climate.

Scientists have calculated that a population needs at least 50 breeding individuals to avoid the negative effects of inbreeding depression and at least 500 breeding individuals to avoid loss of genetic diversity through genetic drift. The required population size becomes even higher if we include the effects of different breeding systems, fluctuations in sex ratio, changes in the age structure of a group, outbreak of disease, climatic conditions and a host of other chance events that can befall a population. These factors, taken together, determine the long-term viability of a population and conservation scientists have expended much effort to develop tools to assess this. Perhaps the best-known is 'population viability analysis' – a sophisticated computer model which estimates the probability of a population surviving over a given time period (often 1,000 years). Another popular method is to calculate the 'minimum viable population' needed to give a high probability of surviving for a long period of time.

Scientists have also converted concepts about declining populations and small populations into a set of categories and criteria that assign a probability of extinction to a species within a time-scale meaningful both to conservationists and policy makers. The International Union for the Conservation of Nature (IUCN) defines a species as extinct if 'there is no reasonable doubt that the last individual has died'. While this definition clearly characterises the state of being extinct, it falls far short of capturing the significance and meaning of 'extinction'. Only, perhaps, when conservationists have an expanded understanding, which includes the ways in which different cultures and organisations respond to the threat of extinction, will we achieve a genuinely predictive theory of extinction, or more usefully, of avoiding extinction.

Applied conservation science

Science plays an important role in measuring and assessing changes in species and habitats and in designing new and innovative ways to deal with conservation problems, uncovering important details about the natural world and the rate of destruction that follows in the wake of civilisation.

Applied conservation science: monitoring and assessing species

How many species are there in the world? This is one of conservation's most basic and fundamental questions but one that is difficult to answer, due to technological and practical limits. Many currently 'unknown' species are residents of tropical forests; the same forests that are being cut down at an alarming speed. It is very likely that many species become extinct before science is even aware of them. However, not yet being discovered does not mean they are ignored by the global conservation movement: every time you hear or read about 'x' species going extinct every day, that number more than likely includes the huge, undifferentiated number of the 'yet to be discovered'.

Due to the imperfect state of scientific knowledge, there are two answers to the question. Ignoring bacteria and viruses, for which the concept of species does not apply in a conventional sense, the first answer is the number of species that have been scientifically described, which is just under two million. There is little point in trying to be more precise; many species appear more than once (under different names) while others are wrongly grouped into a single species. This is not due to the incompetence or carelessness of present-day taxonomists (scientists who specialise in identifying, naming and classifying new species) – many species were described decades or centuries ago. Due to lack of government funding, there are currently very few taxonomists left, especially those of the quality needed to sort out the more complex groups whose specimens litter the great museums of the world. The lack of technical capacity to identify and classify unusual species was highlighted in Britain in November 2008, when it was revealed that only eight professional mycologists (experts on fungi) remained in the UK – and most of them were approaching retirement. The situation is often a lot worse in the developing world, home to the majority of the world's undiscovered species.

The second answer to the question is somewhere between 10 million and 100 million. The enormous range in this answer is due to disagreements over the rate of discovery of new species and how easily this can be extrapolated to the millions of acres of habitat that have not been properly surveyed. We do know there are a lot of new species waiting to be discovered: since the mid-1990s, scientists working in the Mekong delta in South East Asia have found on average two new species a week, including twenty-two new species of snake. Nor are discoveries of new species confined to tropical rainforests and exotic locations. In 1998, a previously unknown giant lizard species was found on a

Figure 10 Fogging (spraying trees with insecticide) is one of the main methods of discovering new species of insect in tropical forests

rocky ridge between the tourist traps of Las Americas and Los Cristianos on the island of Tenerife. It is hard to know which is more amazing: that a species of lizard over 30cm long had remained unnoticed on a small island with nearly a million human inhabitants or that these remarkable creatures had tenaciously clung on to existence while surrounded by a horde of 3.5 million British and German tourists.

Despite the lack of taxonomists and the (potentially huge) number of species to be identified, there are good reasons to be optimistic about the ability of science and technology to fill this gap in our knowledge. A new field of study is emerging: *bioinformatics,* the development of tools and techniques for storing, handling and communicating massive, and ever-increasing, amounts of biological information. Serious attempts are currently being made to develop computer programs that have the ability to learn to identify species from digital images. In principle, it is possible to 'train' this type of program to identify species from images and thus recognise new species, for which no records exist. Another tool that may speed up identification of new species is 'DNA bar-coding': the identification of short but unique sections of a species' genetic profile. Such technology exists and is being used in a limited way: a group of scientists recently identified DNA barcodes for 260 of the 667 North American bird species. However, both these new methods are currently most useful as supplements to traditional taxonomy.

If these – and other – new technologies can be developed and fully exploited, we could see an explosion in the amount of information available about life on Earth. But information is only useful if it can be easily retrieved and processed: again, technology is giving conservationists powerful tools. Probably the most ambitious bioinformatics project is the *Encyclopedia of Life* (www.eol.org), whose aim is to 'make available via the Internet virtually all information about life present on Earth'. The project plans to create a website for each of the (approximately) 1.8 million known species, with pages for the general public and more specialised users. The sites for each species will be linked, flexible and constantly updated as new information on ecology, genetics and conservation comes in. The Encyclopedia could be an invaluable resource for conservation if it can improve access to knowledge and improve the quality, accuracy and speed of data collection.

Knowing about the identities and distribution of all the species on Earth is clearly useful but, in the short to medium term, the most important piece of information for conservationists is whether a species is endangered, threatened with extinction or otherwise in vital need of conservation action. Assessing the conservation status of a species means not just knowing about its distribution but also its populations' size, trend, structure and any threat to its long-term survival. The IUCN has defined nine categories to describe a species' conservation status (see Figure 11). One of these categories – 'endangered' – is commonly, but somewhat loosely, used by media, politicians and the public to mean a population or a species that is threatened in some way by human activity. Although conservationists also use it in this generic sense, the technical meaning of

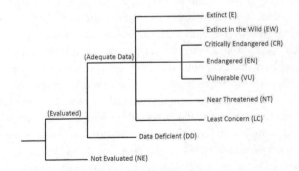

Figure 11 Structure of IUCN Red List categories

'endangered' derives from the famous IUCN Red Lists, which seek to define the conservation status of species (and sometimes populations) to help decide priorities. The IUCN define a species as being endangered if it meets one or more of these criteria:

Very significant reduction in population size: in the range of a greater than 70% reduction in population over any ten-year or three-generation period.

Very significant reduction in geographic area: population restricted to very small areas (less than 5,000 km²), highly fragmented habitats or with large fluctuations in size and range.

Population size estimated to be fewer than 2,500 mature individuals with evidence that the decline is continuing at a rapid rate.

Population size estimated to be fewer than 250 mature individuals.

Quantitative analysis shows the **probability of extinction in the wild is at least 20%** within twenty years or five generations, whichever is the longer (up to a maximum of 100 years).

These criteria are not arbitrary but based on the concepts, theories, experiments and observations of conservation scientists. No complex and universal system, such the Red Lists, can be infallible, whatever the strength of the underlying science. There is constant argument among scientists studying different groups of plants and animals about which category they should be in or whether they should be upgraded (for example, from 'vulnerable' to 'endangered') or downgraded (for example, from 'critically endangered' to 'endangered'). These arguments are normally supported by the interpretation of hard scientific evidence but the Red Lists are also inevitably influenced by personal judgement, environmental politics and the risks of not taking action even without scientific consensus.

Can we now address the fundamental question of how many species are endangered? The IUCN's most recent statistics reveal that there are 2,488 animal and 2,280 plant 'endangered' species. However, a more accurate assessment would include species that are 'critically endangered' and those that are 'vulnerable', which brings the numbers up to 8,462 animal and 8,457 plant species. The distribution of endangered species is unequal between the animal and plant kingdoms: for example, there are far more endangered vertebrate species (mammals, birds, reptiles and amphibians) than any other group (Table 3). This may be a consequence of the considerably better data that are available for bigger, charismatic and culturally important species but probably also reflects the position of these animals at the top of food chains, where they are more vulnerable to ecological disruptions and exploitation. Amphibians (frogs, toads, salamanders and their ilk) are in especially rapid decline, possibly due to a combination of fungal disease and global warming.

One of the many difficulties of conservation monitoring is that it is easier to say a species is endangered than to confirm it has become extinct. The rate of species extinction is a staple of sensationalist newspaper headlines, frequently used as evidence that the world is on the brink of environmental catastrophe. A quick Internet search could net you a startling range of estimates of extinction, from a couple of dozen to over 70,000 species every year. The enormous variation in published figures reflects

Table 3 Summary statistics for endangered and vulnerable vertebrates

	Critically endangered	Endangered	Vulnerable	**Total**
Mammals	188	448	505	**1,141**
Birds	190	361	671	**1,222**
Reptiles	86	134	203	**423**
Amphibians	475	755	675	**1,905**

the enormous scientific uncertainty that surrounds the issue. Part of this uncertainty derives from our imprecise knowledge of the number of species on Earth (see above), part from the difficulty of assessing whether a species has actually become extinct and part from a lack of scientific understanding of the process of extinction. The IUCN Red Lists distinguish between two types of extinction: 'extinct' and 'extinct in the wild'. A species (or population) is considered 'extinct' when there is no reasonable doubt that the last individual has died. By contrast, 'extinct in the wild' means a species may have survived in captivity, cultivation or as a population living well outside its historical geographic range. 'Extinct in the wild' thus includes animals such as the Hawaiian Crow, whose last two wild individuals disappeared in 2002 but groups of which still exist in captive breeding facilities. (The reasons for the crow's extinction are not fully understood but probably included habitat loss, illegal hunting and infectious disease.)

The phoenix-like resurrections of long-extinct species mean that we may one day need to add another category of extinct: species with no living representatives but for which there is genetic material available. Of fifteen known species of giant tortoise from the Galapagos Islands, four have already become extinct. In September 2008, conservation scientists from Yale University, Connecticut, hit the headlines with an announcement that they intended to resurrect an extinct Galapagos giant tortoise, *Geochelone elephantopus*, last seen only fifteen years after Darwin's famous 1835 visit to the archipelago. *Elephantopus's* misfortune was to be native to the island of Floreana – a small, accessible island, attractive to European sailors in search of easily stored meat for the trip home. The Yale scientists found tortoises on Isabella (a larger, more mountainous island to the north-west of Floreana), which contained genes of the extinct species, identified using museum specimens. They believe that an almost 'pure' genetic individual can be created within four (tortoise) generations through careful back-breeding.

Putting aside issues of terminology, the measurement and prediction of extinction rates has always been a matter of considerable interest to conservation scientists. However, it is absolutely dependent on assumptions of how many species there are in the world. The more species we assume to exist, the more can become extinct. This clearly illustrates the need to distinguish between observed extinctions of species already known to science and the extinction of species thought to exist but which have not yet been discovered. The highest estimates for extinction rates (thousands rather than hundreds per year) include this latter category; unfortunate species that blink out of existence before they can make a nameable appearance through a pair of conservationist's binoculars or under a scientist's microscope.

Applied conservation science: monitoring and assessing habitats and ecosystems

Habitats and ecosystems can change in a huge number of ways and one of the main challenges facing conservationists is to decide which elements of a habitat should be monitored. Some talk about ecosystem 'health', where a healthy ecosystem is defined as being both stable and sustainable: maintaining its organisation and autonomy over time and showing a degree of resilience to wider environmental changes. Ecosystems are naturally dynamic but if they are exposed to a high degree of stress (for example, from pollution, climate change, invasive species and so on) their species diversity can reduce rapidly. However, this approach is not universally accepted; many conservationists argue that 'health' cannot be meaningfully attributed to ecosystems and that an ecosystem is simply the sum of the interactions between the species that live there. Whether ecosystems have health or not, it is universally agreed that many are rapidly changing, often with disastrous consequences for the species that inhabit them. The conservationists' job is to monitor and assess these changes in structure and function and, if possible, to distinguish natural change from that caused by human action.

Probably the most fundamental change in ecosystems or habitats is their almost-complete destruction. Such enormous changes are relatively easy to measure and cause the greatest species loss and population decline. The world is seeing this in forests, grasslands and coral reefs. Tropical forests once covered between 14 and 18 million square kilometres but by the late 1980s, only about half that area remained. (Imagine the whole of the North American continent as a single continuous forest, from which humans have removed all the trees covering the USA). And the destruction of tropical forests continues. While the causes of deforestation are well known, the solutions are far more problematic. Most countries with tropical rainforest face enormous economic difficulties. The huge – but constantly shrinking – Amazon forest in South America stretches across more than 6 million square kilometres and nine countries. It is thought that about eighteen per cent of the original forest has been cleared, mainly for agricultural purposes, and that the rate of destruction may be increasing and is certainly not being effectively controlled. Provisional estimates from satellite remote sensing indicated that 25,400 square kilometres of forest was cleared in 2002, compared to an average of 17,340 square kilometres over the preceding ten years. The forest covers 60% of the territory of South America's largest country, Brazil. Here, the main cause of deforestation is well known: beef cattle ranches currently occupy 75% of newly deforested land. And more change will come, as new global markets for products such as soya and biofuels expand.

Advances in technology are also dramatically altering the ways we can assess changes in habitats and ecosystems. Most important is the development of remote sensing: the use of aircraft or satellites to detect land use. Different land uses, such as growing different crops, produce different signals in the electro-magnetic spectrum, which can be identified using sophisticated computer programs. Remote sensing can detect important aspects of the habitat (such as the extent of forest glades or watering holes) from which rough estimates of populations or species can be made. In its early days, remote sensing was a very crude science, typically producing images that averaged information over tens or even hundreds of square metres. However, recent advances in resolution mean that, in some circumstances, individual species of large organisms, such as trees, can be identified.

One day, technology may be developed to the level where remote sensing is used for the majority of both habitat and species assessment. However, that day remains far off; the majority of information on ecosystems, habitats and populations is still compiled in the old-fashioned way by scientists armed with measuring tapes, squares, traps, binoculars, microscopes, and other basic tools. This means the enormous holes in our knowledge about the natural world are closing excruciatingly slowly; a problem that technology is unlikely to solve in the near future. This is a very real difficulty for conservationists: they must make their decisions now, using the data available to them, however incomplete or tenuous they may be.

Applying theory to practice

In many respects, the issue of what the priorities should be and where efforts should be concentrated is the most fundamental in modern conservation. Conservationists have limited resources: it is simply neither possible, nor probably desirable, to protect everything. Some places in the world are more threatened than others and have much greater numbers of endangered species. It makes sense to focus our resources and efforts where they are most needed.

Some international conservation organisations have attempted, with varying levels of success, to create global protected area planning frameworks. There are several schemes, based on different criteria, but they can be grouped into three broad categories: biogeographical representation approaches, which identify examples of ecosystem types using established biogeographic or ecological frameworks; targeting approaches, which identify areas (hotspots) that are either generally rich in species or contain unique species and are under threat (sometimes referred to as the 'silver bullet' approach); and finally, approaches using some other criteria of importance, such as sites of migration or breeding.

Perhaps the best known, and certainly the best funded, of these schemes is Conservation International's biodiversity hotspots approach (see Chapter 3). CI's scientists have currently identified twenty-five hotspots (areas that possess greater than 1.5% of global plant diversity and which have lost more than 70% of their original habitat) as priority areas for conservation action. Conservation International claim that these twenty-five areas hold 44% of the world's plant species and 35% of vertebrate species despite occupying only 12% of its land area. The areas delimited are far too coarse-grained for creating actual reserves but nevertheless, hotspots may be a useful tool for identifying the areas and ecosystems most deserving of funding and conservation attention.

Global prioritisation schemes have their critics. Drawing up priorities inevitably involves personal judgements and may result in funds being drawn from other areas of pressing conservation concern. Global planning frameworks are undoubtedly important tools for the vitally important task of persuading governments and international institutions about the urgent need for conservation action and for raising much needed funds but it is debatable whether they genuinely help effective 'on the ground' conservation.

The new science of conservation

Figure 12 Traditionally, conservation organisations have trained students in techniques for taking wildlife censuses but building their capacity to understand how their peers value wildlife and the environment is just as important for successful conservation action (photo © Fahrul P. Amama)

The most recent trend in conservation science is a shift to greater interdisciplinarity; the incorporation of ideas and information from other academic disciplines, especially from the social sciences such as anthropology, sociology, economics and law. There are three reasons for this trend: first, conservationists acknowledge that a biological understanding of rarity and endangerment, while necessary, is not sufficient, on its own, to effectively prevent the loss of species and habitats. Conservation involves engaging with the messy real world of politics, economics and people. Ideas and concepts developed in sociology, geography, economics and anthropology offer powerful ways of thinking about the relationship between nature and society and provide valuable methods for investigating conservation problems. An increasing number of conservationists are embracing social science as a possible route to improving the performance and impact of their work. Second, a consequence of the integration of conservation with intergovernmental development organisations is that many conservation agencies now have personnel trained in the social sciences and humanities, for whom using tools from both disciplines is part of working effectively. Finally, social scientists increasingly see conservation as a legitimate area of study and academic criticism. Conservation scientists are therefore being forced to understand and respond to these new perspectives and ideas and give social scientists space to express their views in academic journals and conferences that traditionally adopted a strictly biological and ecological perspective.

The social sciences have a range of methods that conservation is starting to put to good use. The questionnaire survey is one of the most familiar: enormously useful for checking assumptions, selecting interventions and demonstrating support. For example, it is assumed that farmers whose livestock is falling prey to carnivores will want to be rid of them and that one way to garner support for the conservation of large carnivores is to compensate farmers for the loss of their stock. However, when a group of Slovenian scientists surveyed people living in an area with a large brown bear population, they found that dislike of the bears was, completely understandably, most strongly linked to a fear of personal attack. This (largely unfounded) fear can be effectively addressed through public information campaigns, much cheaper than setting up an unnecessary compensation scheme. In a quite different example, the National Trust in the UK commissioned a survey of public perception of the countryside. Over half of the respondents said that visiting the countryside was either critical or very important to their quality of life. This finding strengthens the National Trust in its lobbying activities – which is, of course, why it asked the question.

Another common research approach in sociology is the interview, which, together with other ethnographic methods, seeks to reveal insights into particular issues, processes and practices. These insights are typically filtered through individual perspectives or theoretical frameworks (essentially different ways of thinking about societies, organisations and individuals) and allow social scientists to uncover aspects of the complexity of human societies that might be important for conservation. For example, assessment and categorisation schemes draw on the ideas of French social theorists who worked on understanding

Figure 13 Millions of people depend on medicinal plants for basic health care. Conservation scientists work with indigenous experts, such as this Tibetan Yamche, to study the distribution and harvesting of medicinal plants to promote sustainable harvesting (photo © Susanne F. Schmitt)

why markets seem to have a life (and rules) of their own. Applying such perspectives to conservation is useful because it enables conservationists to think about what they do in different ways and therefore ask new, and perhaps more sophisticated, questions about why some actions work and others do not, how to exert and wield influence and why certain organisations and groups are critical of the conservation movement.

Social scientists working in environmental politics and environmental governance contribute valuable ideas about the way power is distributed and exercised and how this varies across cultures and at different scales. Such insights enable conservation organisations to develop innovations in response to the changing dynamics of the organisation of society – for example, the rise of free-market economies. Two further disciplines making invaluable contributions to conservation are anthropology and political ecology. Social anthropology, with its emphasis on

Figure 14 Although the scale and impact of illegal logging are well known, many countries still find it difficult to enforce their laws on the ground

interpersonal and intergroup relations in human societies, is transforming community-based approaches to nature conservation across the world. More specialist branches of anthropology study the relationship between traditional cultures and habitats. One of the more important is ethnobotany, which blends thinking from anthropology, botany and natural resource management. Its scientists work with people who have traditional knowledge, for example about the use and management of plants, to devise ways to retain and strengthen that knowledge and ensure the sustainable use of natural resources in the face of social change and other external pressures.

Political ecology, the study of the interaction between the environment and political, economic and social power systems, generates important new ways of thinking about conservation: for example on the role of the environment in shaping and changing systems or the role of systems in creating and defining environment issues. Insights from political ecology are helping to build a richer and more subtle understanding of major threats such as illegal logging and tropical deforestation, and to provide explanations for why some governments find it difficult to live up to their own conservation rhetoric.

In the 1980s, young people who wanted to pursue a career in conservation were advised to study ecology, zoology or environmental science. Nowadays, the schools they can follow are (or should be) more eclectic. Many disciplines feed modern conservation; exciting advances are likely come at the junctions of the natural and social science perspectives. These changes are reflected in the recent growth of interdisciplinary post-graduate courses in conservation that recruit students from the sciences, the social sciences and the humanities. The infusion of new ideas, new perspectives and new conservationists able to work across and between traditional disciplinary boundaries is certain to have a huge influence on twenty-first century conservation.

5
Taking action

Ultimately, conservation is about making a difference; having a positive influence on the status of a species, site, habitat or a landscape. The influence-building and scientific activities we have described are ways of maintaining and restoring the nature we value. In this chapter, we will introduce the main spheres of conservation action, beginning with sites and focusing on the bases on which conservation actions are designed and decisions made. Sites – protected areas, to give them their generic name – are critical to conserving species and habitats and the foundation of landscape-scale conservation initiatives.

Protecting sites: the backbone of conservation

Protected areas are the backbone of conservation action and the main means through which conservation values are achieved. The number and area of protected areas started to increase, almost exponentially, in the 1970s but the rate has levelled off. In 1962, there were about 1,000 protected areas in the world; by 2004, there were approximately 108,000, covering an area of 11.75 million square miles, just over 12% of the Earth's land area. Conservationists rightly consider this a huge achievement, although one that has been bought at a high social cost (see Chapter 7). There are far fewer marine protected areas; governments have shown much less interest in this environment. Not until 2009 did the UK government finally pass a Marine Bill, containing provisions to create a network of reserves around the British coast.

'Protected area' is something of a catch-all phrase, applied to land that has been allocated by states or bought by private interests with the primary (or compatible secondary) function of conserving the attributes of nature that a society values. Underneath this umbrella shelter a huge array of names and terms applied to a specific site: national park, wildlife refuge, nature reserve and more. Some protected areas have multiple names or designations, because the definitions applied to protected areas arise from their purpose, legal definition and degree of protection, all of which change and vary among countries and at different levels of government.

In the early days of the conservation movement, when many different agendas were articulated, the purpose of protected areas was explicit in their nomenclature. In the late nineteenth century, the wildlife movement advocated the creation of wildlife sanctuaries and refuges, natural historians bid for nature monuments and nature reserves and activists of the open spaces movement pushed for country parks (UK) and state parks (US). The American wilderness movement pushed for the creation of wilderness areas and wise-use resource managers established game reserves, forest reserves and watershed protection forests. These terms, together with 'national park', are the basic set of protected area types present in much early and subsequent legislation. The number of names for protected areas has massively proliferated as governments seek to create legal frameworks for conservation either individually or as a community of nations. For example, when the British government passed the National Parks and Access to the Countryside Act (1949), it created the title 'Site of Special Scientific Interest' (SSSI) and a government agency responsible for their designation. Crucially, land could be designated as a SSSI whether or not it was in an existing protected area, creating a legislative building block for a site-based nature conservation strategy. Consequently, some nature reserves and national parks (or areas within them), are not SSSI, while many SSSI are in agricultural land but can be considered protected areas.

The same holds for designations established through international convention or European law. The 1972 *Convention Concerning the Protection of the World Cultural and Natural Heritage* (better known as the UNESCO World Heritage Convention) invited countries to propose sites for inclusion on the world heritage list. Many countries proposed their most spectacular,

NATIONAL PARKS

'National park' is the most famous and influential of the early reserve types, yet the purpose of national parks is not self-evident from the name. Many national parks began as wildlife sanctuaries or nature monuments. National parks represent the alignment of one or more of the other reserve types (and their conservation values) with efforts to create or reinvigorate a sense of national identity. This is why national parks vary so much among countries. In America, their goal was to use the grandeur and sense of pristine nature to construct national pride and identity, through the creation of Yosemite, Glacier and the other national parks. In the UK, national parks were created as part of a policy to redefine a post-colonial identity; they were situated in rural landscapes close to major cities, such as the Lake District and the Yorkshire Dales. In developing countries, such as Indonesia and Madagascar, national parks help to project a favourable international image, attract international funding and potentially strengthen central state control over remote areas. They are a demonstration of a government's commitment to international norms relating to conservation, rational resource management and community empowerment. Conservation NGOs have promoted national parks in developing countries, because there is an acceptance that they will cover larger areas than other reserve types and governments will feel a greater duty to protect and manage them.

existing, national parks – Serengeti (Kenya), Uluru (Australia) and Yosemite (USA). Other countries employed world heritage status designation as a tool for conserving a cultural landscape. This had many advantages, including the mobilisation of local pride, development of a sense of international responsibility and the strengthening of existing planning laws to encourage 'heritage-friendly' development. An example of this approach is the Jurassic Coast World Heritage Site in the south-west of England, which both covers a scenic agricultural landscape and has many small nature reserves nestling within it. Similarly, the European Union's Birds (1979) and Habitats (1992) Directives require member states to identify and designate special protection areas (SPA) and special areas of conservation (SAC). These sites may or may not previously have been managed or legally designated as reserves (for example as a SSSI).

Protected areas may also be named in relation to the degree of protection accorded to the site. This is the origin of terms such as 'gazetted', 'designated' and 'proposed' protected areas. These have most significance in developing countries and where conservation areas are part of a nationalised forest estate. A 'proposed' protected area is one that has been described in official government strategies and pronouncements. For example, when it hosted the World Parks Congress in Bali in 1980, Indonesia declared proposals for twenty national parks but it took eighteen years until the government passed a National Parks Act. A 'designated' protected area is one of which the boundaries are officially mapped and which has a legally binding land use plan. Designation means that a government department may not issue logging or plantation concessions within the mapped boundaries, unless they change their land use plan. Designation is all the protection many forest reserves in remote areas need. 'Gazetting', the enclosing and fencing of reserves, involves a large-scale mapping of boundaries and often the erection of boundary markers, in consultation with local people.

Table 4 IUCN protected areas category

CATEGORY 1a	Strict Nature Reserve: protected area managed mainly for science
Definition	Area of land and/or sea possessing some outstanding or representative ecosystems, geological or physiological features and/or species, available primarily for scientific research and/or environmental monitoring.
CATEGORY 1b	Wilderness Area: protected area managed mainly for wilderness protection
Definition	Large area of unmodified or slightly modified land, and/or sea, retaining its natural character and influence, without permanent or significant habitation, which is protected and managed so as to preserve its natural condition.
CATEGORY 2	National Park: protected area managed mainly for ecosystem protection and recreation
Definition	Natural area of land and/or sea, designation to (a) protect the ecological integrity of one or more ecosystems for present and future generations, (b) exclude exploitation or occupation inimical to the purposes of designation of the area, and (c) provide a foundation for spiritual, scientific, educational, recreational and visitor opportunities, all of which must be environmentally and culturally compatible.
CATEGORY 3	Natural Monument: protected area managed mainly for conservation of specific natural features
Definition	Area containing one or more specific natural or natural/cultural features of outstanding or unique value because of its inherent rarity, representative or aesthetic qualities or cultural significance.
CATEGORY 4	Habitat/Species Management Area: protected area managed mainly for conservation through management intervention
Definition	Area of land and/or sea subject to active intervention for management purposes so as to ensure the maintenance of habitats and/or meet the requirements of specific species.

CATEGORY 5	Protected Landscape/Seascape: protected area managed mainly for landscape/seascape conservation and recreation
Definition	Area of land, with coast and sea as appropriate, where the interaction of people and nature over time has produced an area of distinct character with significant aesthetic, ecological and/or cultural value, and often with high biological diversity. Safeguarding the integrity of this traditional interaction is vital to the protection, maintenance and evolution of such an area.
CATEGORY 6	Managed Resource Protected Area: protected area managed mainly for the sustainable use of natural ecosystems
Definition	Area containing predominantly unmodified natural systems, managed to ensure long-term protection and maintenance of biological diversity, while providing at the same time a sustainable flow of natural products and service to meet community needs.

Without visible boundaries, it is difficult to enforce management rules and restriction through the local courts; infringers could reasonably argue that they were unaware they were within a protected area.

The – somewhat derogatory – term 'paper parks' was coined by conservationists as a means to embarrass governments into action, by implying that their current levels of park management are ineffective or non-existent. In a paper park, the protected area exists in official documents and reports (on paper) but its physical reality is no different from that of an unprotected site.

If all this were not confusing enough, the IUCN has a long-established system for categorising protected areas that it uses to generate international statistics (see Table 4). This system groups protected areas into six management categories, which necessarily is a somewhat simplified representation. It is based on an implicit hierarchy of human presence and intervention, which some developing countries have used as a basis for their national legislation.

Governing protected areas

A new focus of conservation interest revolves around how protected areas are governed. The World Commission on Protected Areas defines governance as the 'interactions among structures, processes and traditions that determine how power is exercised, how decisions are taken on issues of public concern and how citizens or other stakeholders have their say'. In short, how decisions are taken, who takes them and who is accountable to whom. Many important decisions must be made about protected areas, entailing different powers and responsibilities: where a reserve should be, who has a role in its management, what its management goals will be, what rules will be applied and to whom, who will enforce the rules, how management budgets will be allocated and how the funds will be generated.

Most protected areas are managed by governments but the number of private reserves and community conservation areas is increasing. Many government conservation bodies also now engage with partners for the governance and management of protected areas. This trend reflects the fashion for less government control, the involvement of business and civil society in the delivery of public goods and the growing complexity of protected area management. In the early days, most governments took the view that only they possessed the authority and capacity to manage reserves more than a few hectares in size and thus that protected area and conservation delivery should be their responsibility. The state-owned national park, wildlife sanctuary or nature reserve is the most common protected area model, particularly in countries where forest lands have been nationalised at some stage (such as Indonesia, Vietnam and Russia), countries with a colonial legacy (for example Tanzania and Kenya) or those with large land areas that lacked legal title in the recent past (such as the USA, Canada, Australia and South Africa). In Europe's more densely populated and ancient cultural landscapes, it was harder and more expensive for governments to acquire land so they have generally pursued other strategies. State-owned protected areas fall under the juris-diction of a government body, either a department within a ministry or a government agency. Regional or municipal governments operate similar models. A large protected area is likely to have its own management, headed by a director and with finance, legal and policy issues, enforcement, science and recreation management departments. Smaller protected areas are usually jointly managed from a regional office, with one or more site managers working in the area.

The Kruger National Park, in South Africa, is a superb example of a modern state-managed protected area and the flagship of the South African tourism industry. It is managed by SANParks – a government agency created during post-apartheid restructuring to manage all national parks. SANParks has devel-oped a range of partnerships that provide the resources, skills, insights and support needed to tackle some major management issues. A key challenge is how to make the Kruger relevant to black South Africans, not just to the million white, middle-class South Africans and foreign tourists who visit it every year. To poor black people, especially those living on its boundaries, the Kruger could easily symbolise the continuation of social divisions and injustice. Other key issues include the question of whether the elephant population should be culled, whether fire should be managed and perhaps most importantly, how to make the park financially viable. SANParks works with leading universities to develop 'adaptive management' that embraces a dynamic and flexible approach to wildlife and landscape management and which can incorporate people and their inter-actions with landscape. A unique body, the People and Conservation Directorate, exists to foster stronger relations between the communities surrounding the park and the wider African public. Joint management forums have been created to involve neighbouring communities in decision-making, many people from surrounding villages are employed in the park and strategies are being developed to increase the number of black South African visitors.

Increasingly, as greater democracy and decentralisation recognise old land entitlements, protected areas are being governed through 'multi-actor management' organisations. These create opportunities for diverse interest groups to have a legitimate say in how they are managed. Such management methods typically involve complex governance arrangements, sharing responsibility and authority among groups who may operate at different scales and have very different management goals. The French *parcs naturels regionaux* (PNR) system is a successful example of multi-actor management. The *parcs* were designed to conserve rural areas with a special natural, cultural and human heritage and to develop this heritage sensitively and sustainably. Their core is a partnership between the national Environment Ministry and regional and local government. The state does not decide the location of PNR; rather, the government invites lower levels of administration to apply for a PNR 'seal'. The seal is a mix of the *appellation d'origine contrôlée* system that assures product origin, and an eco-label. It puts a region on the tourist map, enhances its ability to secure European development funds, creates jobs and draws gifted young professional people into rural areas.

The PNR seal is issued against a charter, drawn up by a team of elected representatives, government officials, NGOs and businesses from the proposed PNR. The charter is a ten-year, renewable contract that establishes the park's goals, broadly outlines the actions needed to achieve them and denotes the organisations responsible for their implementation. The PNR model promotes commitment from key local institutions and strengthens professional capacity in the region. Day-to-day management is the responsibility of fifteen to twenty staff, either assigned to the PNR by the local government or employed specifically for their technical expertise. Each park is governed by a committee of elected representatives from regional and local government and the town, supported by an advisory committee drawn from the team who created the charter. The charter, and detailed management plans, bind the three elements together. The PNR model has proved both popular and effective: the PNR *Fedération* currently boasts 45 members and the model is being adopted by other countries, particularly in Eastern Europe.

Another leading example of co-management is the Australian indigenous protected areas. In 1992, the Federal Government of Australia decided to establish a comprehensive, adequate and representative system of protected areas for Australia. However, scientific analysis of where additional reserves were needed found that many areas with a high priority for conservation were owned by indigenous Australians. Around the same time, the Australian High Court gave legal recognition to existing aboriginal 'native title' in disputes over land. The staff of the state conservation agencies took a pragmatic approach and, after talking to indigenous leaders and reviewing the laws covering conservation on private lands, found that there was considerable overlap between the aspirations of indigenous land management and the purpose of protected areas. Indeed, aboriginal Australians expressed a strong desire to maintain the landscapes that were an important part of their cultural heritage.

The result was the creation of Indigenous Protected Areas (IPAs), a new type of protected area for Australia. IPAs are voluntary and declared by the relevant indigenous group but approval relies on government acceptance of a management plan, developed by the indigenous group in close consultation with territory, state and federal conservation agencies. The first IPA was created in Nantawarrina, Southern Australia in August 1998. A further 24 have since been declared. As well as generating new employment opportunities for indigenous peoples, IPAs also allow valuable traditional and scientific management knowledge to flow between indigenous communities and conservation scientists.

It is widely recognised that many wildlife-rich landscapes are the direct result of humans' interactions with their environment. However, in many cases, the traditional practices that created these landscapes have been eroded by authoritarian states, markets and environmental degradation or a combination of all three. In response, conservationists have created 'Community Conserved Areas', where they seek to rebuild and reinvigorate community-level institutions with the authority and capacity to manage their natural resources sustainably. A leading example is the 'Communal Conservancy' model, developed in Namibia, and now being adopted in other African countries. This model was founded on the belief that if communities have exclusive rights to use wildlife resources, they will manage the resource sustainably. In 1996, Namibia introduced legislation giving communal area communities the rights to manage wildlife. These powers are administered by a local management institution (the conservancy), which has a committee drawn from the community, a constitution, management goals, a protocol for monitoring and a local mandate under which conservancy management staff operate. To help this process, external conservation groups, such as WWF and the International Institute for Environment and Development (an independent policy research unit) provide technical input, training and general support. Devolving authority over wildlife and tourism to local communities seems to be working well. Populations of cheetah, leopard, wild dog, springbok and zebra in conservancy areas have risen and hundreds of jobs for field officers, community game guards, community resource monitors and office staff have been created. In 2006, it was estimated that approximately US$2.4 million of new money had flowed into conservancy areas since their creation. The fifty legally registered communal conservancy areas now cover nearly 40% of common land in Namibia, with a combined area of about 11.8 million hectares.

Many protected areas are privately owned and can normally be managed with few external constraints. These areas, owned or leased by individuals, business or NGOs, are vital to the conservation movement. This approach has ancient origins, in the private hunting reserves traditionally kept by monarchs and aristocrats. In private reserves, the authority and responsibility for management rests solely with the landowner and decisions are made privately. This means that conservationists can pursue their management vision relatively unencumbered by the need to balance the agendas of many interested parties or to follow strict management regimes imposed by government scientists and bureaucrats. Usually the reserve manager prepares a management plan in consultation with technical staff, government conservation agencies and other statutory agencies (for example water authorities). While there may be some consultation with local landowners there is often little substantial consultation with the organisation's members or regular visitors to the reserve.

On private reserves, conservationists have the freedom to innovate, engage with the public and build a wider policy influence. Perhaps the most familiar type of private reserves are those owned by conservation NGOs. In the UK, the Wildlife Trusts and RSPB own around 2,200 and 150 reserves respectively. In the USA, the Nature Conservancy owns 1,300 reserves, ranging in size from 1.3 to 130,000 hectares; their combined area of well over half a million hectares makes them the world's largest private nature reserve system. Many private reserves are acquired to protect habitats that are disappearing from the wider landscape due to changes in farming practices. These reserves often require intensive and detailed management to maintain their conservation value. Increasingly, conservation groups are buying farmland and restoring past landscapes, connecting or enlarging small habitat patches or designing 'super-habitats' through carefully designed planting. A second type of private protected area, frequently associated with a grand vision, is those that owe their existence to the passion of fabulously wealthy individuals. Douglas Tompkins, co-founder of the retail fashion companies North Face and Esprit, has bought large areas of Chile and Argentina to protect and restore to pristine wilderness. With total land holdings of around 800,000 hectares, he is one of the largest private landowners in the world. Tompkins's vision is to donate the land as national parks, provided the governments agree to keep them untouched in perpetuity. In the USA, Ted Turner, media mogul and founder of CNN, has purchased two million hectares of land, to which he is introducing native species. The ranch now supports 45,000 bison. In Scotland, Paul Lister, heir of the MFI furniture empire, bought five Highland glens and two rivers, which he aims to return to their wild state of three centuries ago, replete with wolves, moose and wild boar.

These private conservation initiatives are not without controversy. Tompkins' Pumalín Park divides Chile in two from the Pacific to the border with Argentina. Big commercial interests, relating to salmon fishing and timber had hoped to develop these lands and politicians wanted to drive a road through it. These interests see foreign land holdings of this scale as a threat to national sovereignty. Paul Lister's vision has required the construction of a massive fence around his property. Walkers condemn his activities as a blot on the landscape, a threat to the recent and hard-won 'right to roam' and as evoking memories of the eighteenth-century Highland clearances carried out by absentee English landlords.

Sub-Saharan Africa also has a growing number of private game and nature reserves. Some cover more than 10,000 hectares and most, if not all, are run commercially. These private reserves offer an exclusive African experience involving luxury lodges and camps, private guides, and trackers to help clients to get the perfect photo or memorable shot. The resilient popularity of trophy hunting means that, in many areas, managing game reserves represents a viable alternative to cattle ranching and one

THE RSPB'S 'FOREST OF HOPE'

Impertinent conservationists used to ask forestry officials: *if companies can lease a forest to log, why can't we lease one to conserve*? The curt answer was that forest concessions are a package of lease fee and tax payment per tree cut; conservation cannot provide the latter. Prompted by a very bleak prognosis for the future of Sumatra's super-diverse lowland rainforests, a consortium including the RSPB, BirdLife International and Burung (formally Birdlife) Indonesia decided to try a different approach. They argued that, rather than contributing tax revenue, they could restore the timber value of a logged forest concession to be a state asset. The Indonesian Ministry of Forestry agreed to the idea of a 'restoration' concession and a BirdLife/RSPB team worked with it for three years to make the required revisions to forest law. BirdLife and the RSPB then formed a company that successfully bid one million pounds for the right to hold 51,000 hectares of a 100,000 hectare ex-logging concession for fifty-five years. They received the licence in 2008 and are now working to secure a concession covering the remainder of the forest block.

As well as restoring the forest, the challenge is to protect the concession from settlers. This may prove difficult. Working against the RSPB and BirdLife are organised gangs selling settlement opportunities to Sumatra's landless peasants. The RSPB and BirdLife are hoping to protect the forest through investing in community development projects, employing rangers from the local community and enlisting the support of the local police and district government. In the past, logging companies were powerless against these powerful networks and entered into a 'race for timber'. Only time will tell whether the NGOs will have more luck with their latest venture.

that, broadly, benefits wildlife. The Shamwari Game Reserve in South Africa is one of the most famous examples. It was created in 1991 by businessman Adrian Gardiner, who bought and consolidated several over-grazed stock farms, which exterminated the feral goats and helped the original vegetation and animals recover. Today, it is a luxurious retreat with six lodges where the wealthy can enjoy Africa's famous mega-fauna and abundant birdlife away from the crowds in the national parks. In South Africa, the area of private game reserves now exceeds that of state-owned protected areas.

Protected areas in context

This overview cannot hope to do justice to the variety of protected areas either in terms of the nature they protect or the ways they are governed or managed. The goals of management of protected areas include nature and landscape conservation, science, outdoor recreation and tourism, livelihood development and the support of indigenous and traditional ways of life. The tools employed include planning, regulation, branding, direct habitat and wildlife management, restoration and re-stocking, partnership and contracting agreements and fund-raising and revenue-generating activities. For many conservation-minded people, working in protected areas is an ideal job, combining variety and a connection to the land with long-term vision. Protected areas are also becoming more politically sensitive, as the burgeoning global population places ever-increasing demands on limited natural resources. Furthermore, protected areas policy has become a domain in which groups concerned with social justice and the rights of marginalised people can make their voices heard. The increasing criticism of conservation practices that appear élite and exclusionary are starting to tarnish the image of protected areas in the eyes of some policy-makers.

Managing habitats

How much conservationists manage habitats depends on their size and how much they have been transformed from their natural state. For some, reserves should protect 'pristine' habitats, exhibiting pre-human species abundance and distribution and which are large enough for nature to 'take its course' with little management. Quite apart from this being an unrealistic ideal in most countries, many species-rich habitats, worthy of conservation, are the product of centuries of low-intensity agricultural management. Most habitats need some management to retain their conservation value.

Habitat management is a particular preoccupation in Europe, where a long agricultural history and dense populations mean there is very little original habitat left. The nature valued by most Europeans is, unsurprisingly, that produced by the long interaction of culture with landscape. Many commentators note that European conservation aspires to a pre-mechanised landscape, last seen somewhere around the 1850s and that frequently, the management's purpose is to retain patches of these historic landscapes. The best, or increasingly only remaining, examples of these habitats have been preserved as nature reserves, subject to detailed management prescriptions, devised to keep (or restore) the site to a 'favourable' conservation condition. Favourable, in this context, means a situation in which habitat and species closely resemble what we imagine them to have been like in the past, based on historic descriptions and classifications, comparison with other remaining examples and – frequently – the traditions and intuition of conservation managers. This type of management is often referred to as 'compositionalist', meaning that it focuses on the identities (composition) of the species present. This approach fits well with governments' enthusiasm for targets and indicators. The mix of species in grassland, or the range and number of breeding waders supported by a wet grazing meadow, can easily be counted and reported and scientists can create simple models of the habitats which can be converted into management prescriptions.

Retaining relict habitat patches often involves reproducing or mimicking pre-industrial land management. Compared to modern agriculture, pre-industrial practices were characterised by lower intensity farming, more extensive, and seasonal, patterns of cropping and grazing implemented by a large rural labour force and using organic rather than chemical fertilisers. The extent to which historical agriculture can be reproduced depends on the habitat and practice in question. For example, the effect of scything hay meadows is easily reproduced with mechanical cutters; the effect of grazing on swards is a little more difficult, because modern cows are bred to graze on lush grassland. To reproduce sward-grazing, managers need to use old breeds, which means either maintaining a herd or finding a sympathetic farmer with an interest in conservation. Conservation organisations cannot normally afford to employ their own teams for labour-intensive agricultural practices such as hedge-laying, reed-cutting, clearing ditches and dykes and herding – old skills which created the species-rich habitats we seek to protect – instead relying on contracted managers working with volunteer teams. However, as reserves increase both in size and number it is more and more difficult to find and organise enough volunteers to keep on top of natural environmental change. Ironically, reserve management is becoming more mechanised as managers look for technological solutions that mimic old practices: using mechanical diggers to create low-maintenance dykes, flailing hedges in specific ways to mimic laid hedges, spot-spraying invasive species and harrowing to recreate the effects of cattle's hooves. These techniques are favoured on rural reserves that do not attract many volunteers and, in particular, on newly created reserves, where increasing biodiversity over-rides improving the quality of visitors' experiences.

The need for highly intensive management is well illustrated in many small heathland reserves in southern England. Heathland is a strange habitat, which exists only during the transition from one type (open grassland or scrub) to another (woodland). Before human agriculture, heathland plants and animals would only have been present in forest clearings, cliffs and other marginal habitats. This changed when humans built herds of animals that grazed the landscape intensively. By the Middle Ages, nearly all the drier areas of southern England were covered in heathland. However, since the 1800s, there has been a steep decline in small-scale farming and the formerly vast southern heathlands have, inevitably, started to return to forest (or, more frequently, forests of houses!).

Managers of heathland reserves have no choice but to reproduce the qualities of peasant farming to maintain heaths as habitats suitable for rare species such as smooth snakes and Dartford warblers. Some site managers do it by controlled burning and organised 'heath-bashing' days, in which volunteers pull up the gorse, birch and bracken that herald the return to woodland. Studland Bay Nature Reserve, in Dorset, has recently hired a cowherd, who grazes the herd where it is needed (and, equally importantly, keeps the cows from being hit by cars speeding towards the ferry). This forward-thinking strategy is popular with the community and makes a lot of sense. If you want to maintain a medieval landscape, what could be better than hiring a 'professional' peasant? A highly desirable job for many stuck in the urban sprawl!

Elsewhere in Europe, the issue is not so much reproducing past management skills as retaining or restoring the markets that promoted the practices that created wildlife-rich landscapes. The Spanish *dehessas*, descendants of the original oak forests of Spain, produced two products – cork for wine bottles and ham from the black pigs that grazed on the acorns. Unfortunately, wine manufactures are turning to plastic corks and screw tops. WWF has a long-standing campaign to encourage wine manufactures, retailers and consumers to stick with cork to avoid the collapse of the *dehessas* economy and their conversion to agriculture.

The constraints facing conservation managers mean that, to a greater or lesser extent, reserves differ from their nineteenth-century counterparts. As well as the difficulty of achieving the outcomes they want with the things they are able to do, managers need to take care of the wider landscape, much of which is beyond their control. Conservation organisations have lawyers working to influence agricultural policy, so that farmed habitats become richer in wildlife and a less 'hostile' matrix in which reserves are embedded. Since the late 1990s, in the developed world, agricultural land has been bought and restored as wildlife habitats that either extend or link existing reserves or create 'stepping stones' to connect isolate populations and promote recolonisation. The Great Fens Project in Cambridgeshire has gradually bought and restored more than 3,000 hectares of farmland between two of England's oldest wetland reserves, Holme and Wood Walton Fens.

The need to maintain or restore viable populations of rare species, or provide 'stop-over' sites along migration routes, means that specially designed reserves must be created. Some are fashioned from scratch, while others are modified to offer the ideal breeding or feeding conditions for the species of interest. The RSPB's efforts to increase the size of the bittern population involves both these approaches: existing reed beds have been extended in bittern strongholds in East Anglia and Somerset and new systems have been specially created on former agricultural land at Lakenheath in Cambridgeshire and Otmoor in Oxfordshire.

Restoring agricultural land, whether to a semblance of a former habitat or a 'super-habitat' serving an endangered species, is fraught with difficulty: agriculture leaves a legacy of compacted soil, high nutrient levels and altered hydrology.

THE SITE MANAGER: CONSERVATION'S GREAT CONNECTOR

Once called wardens, the modern reserve or site manager has the ability to blend, balance and negotiate the range of interests, regulations and physical forces affecting a site. A site manager needs to integrate the views of scientific, policy and marketing colleagues in their organisation, attend to the advice of government conservation agencies and negotiate with the local and national government agencies responsible for planning, water extraction, flood defences and tourism. Crucially, a site manager must diplomatically deal with, and if possible accommodate, the interests of recreational groups, landowners and the local council. A key responsibility is to prepare (or update) and implement a reserve management plan, which provides the framework for consultation, negotiation and agreed management objectives.

The site manager is the classic 'jack of all trades'. In any one day, they might get an email from a politician, discuss management techniques with a colleague, supervise a contractor on the site, chat with a volunteer group, lead a guided walk and deal with building and access problems. The best site managers build a deep affection for their site, both through their work, and observing and recording wildlife. This 'sense of place' enables managers to intuitively and effectively juggle the complex web of human and non-human interactions around a site and to speak compellingly for the site and its wildlife with a blend of expertise, passion and commitment.

Despite the variety, and the enviable mix of outdoor and office work, the job has an image problem and it is becoming increasingly difficult to recruit young managers. Talented conservationists are not sure whether it is a manual or professional job, it is poorly paid and with apparently little opportunity for career progression. Perhaps it is time to resurrect – and give new meaning to – 'Warden'.

When agriculture stops, the land is vulnerable to rapid invasion by undesirable species. New reserves are carefully designed, drawing on a blend of ecology, agricultural know-how and conservation science. These new reserves are the modern equivalents of eighteenth-century landscape gardens, in which people sought to evoke an idealised form of nature and embed political and cultural ideas of society's relationship with nature.

Increasingly, compositionalist approaches are complemented by 'functionalist' or 'process-orientated' approaches, whose aim is to restore important ecological and environmental processes, such as nutrient and water cycling. These processes are often instrumental in providing essential 'ecosystem services' to local communities: for example, recharging of aquifers, pollination of crop plants and erosion control. More and more, conservationists seek to identify and restore these key processes, to enhance the capacity of ecosystems to withstand or adapt to the impacts of accelerated climate change. The debate over fire management in the forests of west coast America and the Australian savannah is one of the clearest examples of the functionalist approach. For many years, reserve managers suppressed fires, fearing they would wipe out the species and habitats they had worked so hard to conserve and create eyesores that would put off visitors. Conservationists now realise that natural fires, sparked by lightning, will, if suppressed, either create forests and savannah very different from the original or lead to the build up of débris and risk unnaturally intense and damaging future fires. Many managers now use controlled burning to mimic the natural process.

Conservationists managing large reserves have always favoured 'letting nature take its course', emphasising ecosystem processes and functions. The Dutch are well ahead in this field; since the 1980s, they have forged an ambitious plan to link their remaining natural areas with a green infra-structure of corridors and byways. They are also trying to restore dynamic ecologies in some of their major rivers by buying agricultural land within large river bends and removing the summer dykes. The UK Wildlife Trusts have launched a 'living landscape' initiative, which they describe as a call to restore the UK's battered ecosystems for wildlife and people. This is essentially a conceptual move, from site- to landscape-scale thinking, explicitly considering the valley, mountain or delta in which a nature reserve is located. It involves understanding the ecological processes that create the conditions for wildlife-rich habitats and looking for ways to restore or manage them better; buying land, influencing the planning system and, perhaps most importantly, working with the government to integrate agriculture, water, road-building and housing policies. The underlying argument is that a focus on function benefits the whole of society, not just nature-lovers.

Landscape approaches to conservation are beginning to incorporate the language of adaption to climate change. Stephanie Holborne, CEO of the UK Wildlife Trusts, describes creating 'climate corridors' that allow wildlife to move up and down the country to shadier slopes or cooler valleys. The Dutch plan for a network of ecological corridors is one means of counteracting the effects of climate change but one likely to be too ambitious for most countries. Elsewhere, managing the movement of animals and plants is framed in terms of enhancing the landscape's 'permeability' to wildlife. This involves a broad approach, of numerous small improvements in connectivity, made wherever the opportunity arises, such as restoring hedgerows or the vegetation at the edges of waterways.

In most developed countries, a functionalist perspective tends to guide larger scale landscape management, while the compositionalist approach dominates site or habitat management. This distinction may start to blur, as new ecological ideas gain a foothold and as the effects of climate change become apparent. The Dutch have taken the functionalist process down to site

scale in the Oostvaarderplassen initiative to reinstate large herbivores as a tool for restoring ecological processes. In the UK, two
classic 'compositionalist' reserves, the RSBP's Titchwell Marsh
and the Norfolk Wildlife Trust's Cley Marsh, are moving
towards more dynamic and uncertain management, because it is
no longer feasible to maintain the massive gravel banks that have
kept the sea at bay for decades.

Species management

Safeguarding sites is only one part of the suite of activities
needed to halt or reverse declines in the populations of wild
species. Reserves might be too small to sustain viable breeding
populations of rare species, conditions within a reserve change,
people poach species or animals unhelpfully wander beyond
their prescribed boundaries. Conservationists do not only want
to conserve species in designated areas but also in the wider
human-dominated landscape. As well as improving the quality
of a habitat for specific species or groups of species, there are a
number of more direct approaches that can ensure a rare species
does not become extinct. Perhaps the most radical is to capture
wild individuals and begin a captive breeding programme, with
the aim of reintroducing the species back into the wild or
supplementing small wild populations. This, together with
environmental education, is the main justification for the
continued existence of zoos and safari parks.

   Although captive breeding and reintroduction seems like an
excellent solution to current conservation problems, it is not
without drawbacks. One of the most serious is the slow,
cumulative effect of natural selection. Over several generations,
those individuals that are most suited to life in captivity will tend
to reproduce at a relatively higher rate, eventually leading to a
population that is tamer and less resistant to disease than the wild

counterparts. There is no way to avoid this completely, although its effects can be reduced by occasionally adding wild-caught individuals to the captive stock (of course, if the population is very rare to begin with, this may be considered a poor strategy). Or the captive environment can be made as natural as possible, although this can have the undesirable effect of making zoo animals in 'realistic' enclosures very hard for the fee-paying public to see. Captive populations are often functionally equivalent to a very small wild population, with all the problems this entails (see Chapter 4). The careful choice of the founding individuals and the co-ordinated management of an international studbook can avoid the worst effects of inbreeding. After some early mistakes, captive breeding programmes are also very aware of the need to maintain the integrity of regional breeding pools to prevent important traits and behaviours being lost. The potential genetic problems of small captive populations can be overcome with careful management but there are some problems associated with captivity that have no easy solutions. Chief amongst these is that large, complex organisms, such as primates and other large mammals, quickly become acclimatised to life in captivity.

The dangers of life in captivity are well illustrated by elephants. In their natural environment, they learn which plants fruit at different seasons and in different environments. They are taught these skills by their mothers, over several years, and the lack of such experience could prove fatal when they are reintroduced to their native environment. In theory, human keepers could train captive elephants in some of these skills but they are unlikely ever to reach the level required for survival in the wild. This passing on of survival and social skills is even more important for species, such as chimpanzees and other primates, with rich and complex social lives. To be accepted into a wild community, as well as knowing how to forage for food, avoid predators and so on, chimpanzees have to learn a wide range of social skills. If they don't have the right social skills, they may be expelled from the group and possibly die. This is why there have been almost no successful reintroductions of the great apes into the wild, especially of animals that were either born in captivity or kept in captivity for a long time. However, despite its many problems, captive breeding remains one of the key methods of avoiding species extinction. Several species, such as the Hawaiian crow, now only exist in captivity; and there are others, such as the black-footed ferret, the Hawaiian goose and the Californian condor, whose continued existence in the wild is attributable to the remarkable and far-sighted efforts of conservationists who took the last remaining wild individuals and, after a successful captive breeding, restored the species to its native environment.

An alternative to captive breeding is 'off-site preservation', in which, to escape from the threats that exist in its native habitat, a species is deliberately introduced into a habitat to which it is not native. This has not been extensively used in conservation, due to the risks associated with introduced species, but may well become more widespread as natural habitats shrink. The Himalayan tahr is a close relative of the wild goat, native to the wooded hills and mountain slopes of the Himalayas stretching from Northern India to Tibet. It is classified as 'vulnerable' by the IUCN Red List. However, feral tahr were introduced to the Southern Alps of the South Island of New Zealand in 1904, where they have bred so successfully that they are now considered a pest, with serious impacts on much of the native vegetation.

The biggest direct threat faced by many spectacular and well-known species (gorillas, elephants, tigers, rhinos and so on) is exploitation by humans for food or, more frequently, economic gain. Saving species often requires a combination of protected areas, enforced legislation, economic incentives, public will and direct intervention. In Chapter 3, we described CITES, the convention created to regulate the trade in wildlife. Creating laws to protect vulnerable species, and ensuring their enforcement, is imperative for species conservation, especially for those species with a market value. The ability of conservationists to enforce laws depends in part on the will and resources of government agencies, in part on who is 'after' the species and in part on whether or not the land is owned by a conservation body.

Game wardens and wildlife rangers epitomise the traditional approach to safeguarding wildlife in reserves. Regular vehicle patrols and surveillance from watchtowers have been critical in the fight to save the world's mega-fauna from extinction. Such actions brought the Indian one-horned rhino and black rhino of Africa back from the brink of extermination. Conversely, the decrease to perilously small levels in the populations of Javan and Sumatran rhinoceros (fewer than 60 and 300 respectively) is partly because it is impossible to mount effective patrols in the dense tropical forests where they live.

'Strict enforcement', as it is often called, is common in many protected areas in Africa, the Indian sub-continent and North America and normal practice for private game reserves where the wildlife has a commercial value. Many Western conservation NGOs lobby their governments to increase policing to stop the persecution of birds of prey and the hunting of rare species and migratory birds. However, in their international operations, many of these same NGOs offer only lukewarm support (at least publicly) for such 'hard' enforcement approaches, because they are seen to run counter to the livelihood and poverty-alleviation agendas that are intertwined with conservation agendas in developing countries. Strict enforcement is costly, unpopular with local communities, ineffective where species are wide-ranging or the threats to it are erratic, and it is easily construed as wealthy outsiders enforcing their values and beliefs on poor rural peasants.

UNDERCOVER INVESTIGATION

Estimates of trade in live animals and animal parts are staggering. Jane Goodall has suggested that 25,000 to 30,000 primates, two to five million birds and ten million reptile skins are exported each year. Small numbers of dedicated conservationists investigate, expose and campaign against the black-market networks, shady individuals and the crimes committed against wildlife and the environment. This is dangerous and disturbing work. Wildlife, guns and drugs all pass through the same underground channels and their buyers include high-ranking army officials, war-lords and criminal bosses.

The Environmental Investigation Agency, an international, independent campaigning organisation, is one of the leading groups in this area. It combines undercover investigations and background research with public campaigns and high-level advocacy. At grave personal risk, its investigators gather film, photos and intelligence using spy-movie surveillance techniques. They employ clear, moral words and phrases in their campaigns – black-market, crime, poachers, underworld, suffering, cruelty and 'culture of killing'. This 'framing' of the issue helps legitimise the 'sting' operations and armed anti-poacher patrols that are a necessary part of their actions.

This area of conservation is sometimes referred to as the 'militarisation of conservation'. In Cambodia the US-based NGO WildAid uses military advisors to train rangers, and armed wildlife patrol units to protect the last refuges of Indo-China's formerly abundant wildlife from armed poaching gangs. Many conservationists working in this field are ex-military: tackling certain aspects of the wildlife trade needs military intelligence and operations skills. And because the wildlife trade is entangled with organised crime, armed insurgency movements and corruption, military and conservation objectives are sometimes blurred.

A regular 'on the ground presence' is usually enough to deter local hunters but wildlife is also targeted by hunters who sell bushmeat at markets and by organised and armed gangs hunting species 'to order', such as rhinos, tigers and bears, with valuable body parts. Dealing with these professional hunters needs military-style intelligence, discipline and patrol methods, not least because many of the hunters themselves are ex-combatants trained in jungle warfare.

Many conservationists advocate 'softer' approaches, based on generating economic or cultural benefits for local communities from the conservation or sustainable use of wildlife and plants. Conservation approaches based on these principles now extend to a range of situations. The CAMPFIRE programme, pioneered during the 1980s in Zimbabwe, looked beyond the simple view that the best solution is to ban the killing of wildlife, and delved deeper into the root causes. They realised that in semi-arid areas wildlife could produce a good income for local people but that these same people were killing crop-raiding animals because there were no clear ways of selling them. CAMPFIRE introduced a set of principles to create markets for wildlife, to give communities ownership of their local wildlife and thus the incentive to manage wildlife populations. In the Philippines, Project Seahorse (seahorse.fisheries.ubc.ca) works with communities, academics and policy-makers to improve the management and sustainable harvesting of seahorses, which are a common ingredient in many traditional Chinese medicines. However, although market-based approaches sound great on paper, experience shows that a number of factors are needed if they are really to make a difference. There must be a cohesive community, willing to take a risk on a new venture, markets willing to be flexible about quantity (and sometimes quality), supportive investors, a natural resource that responds to management and, crucially, talented, entrepreneurial individuals, ready to commit to the enterprise in the medium to long term.

Humans have a long history of persecuting animals through fear or because of competition for resources. Dealing with conflicts between wildlife and humans is a growing challenge for conservationists for two main reasons: first, towns and villages are expanding into natural areas and second, as conservation measures to protect large animals take effect, the animals are extending their range back into areas where they have not been seen for many years. In Europe, people in many areas are being

THE COMPLEX NEXUS BETWEEN CONSERVATION AND DEVELOPMENT

The link between poverty and environmental degradation is well known but finding ways to manage natural resources sustainably while also improving the livelihoods of poor people has proved enormously difficult. The general approach is to invest development aid in new village enterprises (such as ecotourism or bee-keeping) that aim simultaneously to reduce people's reliance on natural resources and create an economic rationale to conserve them. Needless to say, implementing such schemes has proved far more complex than was originally imagined. Members of the community not involved in the new enterprises may continue their unsustainable practices; or, successful enterprises may attract extended family members and migrants to the village, increasing pressure on natural resources. In many cases, trade-offs between conservation and development exist, which cannot be overcome without compensation payments and consideration of local culture and traditions.

The widespread failure of traditional development schemes has led many aid bodies to look towards micro-credit schemes, designed to promote local entrepreneurship. These operate under less paternalistic principles and see poverty as arising partly from a lack of access to affordable, small-scale loans. In an innovative move, the conservation NGO Wetlands International has developed a new mechanism, in which communities receive micro-credits for sustainable enterprises but can repay their loan and interest in conservation services such as reforestation and habitat protection. These 'conservation repayments' are converted into cash, which goes back into a revolving micro-credit fund managed by the community. The beauty of this 'bio-rights approach' is that it translates biodiversity and the natural environment into hard cash for development, creates sustainable village institutions and encourages local entrepreneurs to take the lead in employing or compensating fellow community members for conservation. It has met with notable success in mangrove rehabilitation in Indonesia and harvesting migratory water-birds in the Niger Delta of Mali. However, it does not provide a solution for all poverty/environment issues and must be strongly supported by government policies and planning, especially if external investors are interested in exploiting the resources.

forced to re-learn how to live with large predators after many years, sometimes centuries, of absence. Human–wildlife conflict can mean damage to crops and property, physical injury or even death. The usual suspects are tigers, elephants, wolves and bears. But although less-often discussed, wild boar spilling out from protected areas are a massive problem for many farmers in tropical areas. If conservation groups do not respond to these issues, people will take things into their own hands, which invariably means finding ways to dispose of wildlife. Conservationists' efforts fall into six general categories, often employed in parallel: constructing barriers (for example, fences and ditches), creating deterrents (for example, firecrackers), establishing farmers' compensation schemes, educating people about wildlife so they are better able to live with it, creating corridors and reserves and changing agricultural practices. While the last of these might ultimately be the most effective, it involves people changing their behaviour, which is why it is the most difficult to enact.

The biggest problem is probably human–elephant conflict in India and Africa. Elephants are particularly difficult to deal with because they need large areas to roam in and have exceedingly large appetites. They are also enormously powerful and intelligent and can easily kill people. Moreover, they seem to react to harassment by becoming more aggressive. Indeed, in India, villagers are convinced that elephants take retribution. Deterrents such as spotlights and thunder-crackers are normally the first line of defence. In the last few years experiments have been conducted using chilli powder, pastes, beehives and bombs as deterrents but have met with limited success. Physical barriers, such as electric fences and deep trenches, are widely used but maintenance is a problem and elephants soon learn how to break through; adult male elephants have been observed to push younger males against electric fences. In some areas, farmers are paid compensation in an attempt to quell their anger. However studies suggest that compensation may have the opposite effect, because it requires farmers to make repeated visits to government offices – a frustrating occupation. A more practical approach is devise early-warning devices – simple trip wires and pressure pads – that mean farmers can turn out when elephants arrive, rather than spending tiring nights sitting in watchtowers only for the elephants to raid on the night they miss.

Saving a species is not straightforward. Conservationists need a portfolio of approaches that address the complex mix of direct and indirect threats that sends a species towards extinction. These, together with their underlying rationale, are often set down in a 'species action plan'. These documents are produced through consultation and aim to identify threats and necessary remedial action and to engage the interest of key stakeholders. Species actions plans enable efforts to be co-ordinated, justify specific budget allocations and provide an essential baseline for understanding, which can be developed and refined as the impact of actions is monitored and assessed.

In the UK, species action plans are combined with habitat action plans and local biodiversity action plans to form the UK's Biodiversity Action Plan (www.ukbap.org.uk), the basis of the British Government's response to the 1992 Convention on Biological Diversity (CBD). All countries that signed up to the CBD have developed, or are in the process of developing, a similar approach to conserving species and habitats of conservation concern. The set of approaches and interventions available to conservationists is growing every year and, through international co-operation and communication, conservation has never had so many ways to fight against decline and disturbance. Unfortunately, the need for them has never been so great!

6

Financing conservation

Conservation requires lots of money. Not only money for the protected sites, but money for specialist staff, travel, campaigns and research. In 1999, researchers from the universities of Cambridge and Sheffield estimated that it would cost approximately US$8.3 billion a year to manage the world's protected areas effectively. If the number of conservation areas were expanded to what conservationists consider really necessary (about 15% of the Earth's land surface) it would cost about US$22.6 billion a year to manage and to purchase the new areas. A huge sum – but about the same the world spends on pet food each year and a fraction of the annual US$1.2 trillion global military spending.

Finance for conservation is generated from different sources which can usefully be grouped into three major types: first, unrestricted funds generated by conservation organisations which they can use more or less as they like; second, funds from governments, foundations or other donors for specified purposes; and finally, funds 'released' through the creation of tax breaks or economic devices. Conservation organisations put in a huge amount of effort to generate money from these sources. They have to. They do not make anything, or sell services to make a profit; rather, they promote a vision of a certain type of human relationship with nature and encourage others to contribute to its realisation and maintenance.

Conservation organisations broadly divide into governmental and non-governmental organisations. The first are financed (in part) from governmental budgets. We could say a great deal about the systems and politics that ensure an adequate slice of tax-payers' money goes towards conservation and how this needs to be supplemented by external funds, but this is not our focus in this chapter. Instead, we will concentrate on the financing of conservation NGOs, because they are the organisations most conservation supporters give to or work for as volunteers and staff.

Financing NGOs

Almost everyone connected with a conservation NGO, trustee, employee, member or visitor, is involved with fundraising in some way. Most NGOs employ dedicated fundraisers but project managers are often responsible for raising the bulk of the money for their field activities. An ability to raise funds empowers individual staff with a greater say in what should be done, and how they can build their teams and progress with their careers. Fundraising is also one of the most valuable – and valued – contributions made by volunteers.

To make sense of how conservation organisations finance their operations, we have to understand some key concepts and terminology. The first is the distinction between restricted and unrestricted funds: restricted funds are raised under a contract or agreement that they will be spent on a specific purpose or project. Unrestricted funds have no strings attached and typically are generated through membership fees and donations, retail activities, legacies and endowments. Endowments are gifts of money on which only the interest may be spent. Some US-based conservation NGOs have endowment funds of hundreds of millions and the organisation can spend these funds as it wishes – so long as the activities support its general charitable objectives. Conservation fundraising is quite different in Europe and America: Americans have a much stronger tradition of philanthropic giving compared to Europeans and the USA has many more foundations willing to contribute substantial sums to conservation NGOs. Unrestricted funds are used to pay the 'core costs' of an NGO: salaries and overheads of staff not working on grant-funded projects, such as senior management, administration, fundraising, public relations, office costs and so on. Generating enough money to cover core costs is a major headache for many conservation NGOs, because most donors – understandably – want to fund exciting activities, not people sitting around in offices. An additional problem for fund-raisers is that charity rating organisations (for example guidestar.com and charitynavigator.com) use the ratio of core to operational costs as a key performance indicator – in part because this ratio is easy to calculate from publicly available tax returns.

The art of financing conservation organisations is to maximise unrestricted funds while reducing the perceived cost of core operations. The first means both succeeding in unrestricted fundraising and maximising the overheads and management fees charged on grants and contracts. The second involves negotiating with donors, packaging activities as part of conservation activities and charging the time of core staff to projects wherever possible and appropriate. If a fundraiser opts to send letters or emails to supporters asking them to contribute towards saving a rare Madagascan lemur, the postage or online costs of the appeal could be classified as a conservation-awareness cost, if the letters or emails also contain information on the conservation importance of Madagascar, the uniqueness of lemurs and the threats they face.

Overheads are the costs an organisation can charge a donor (such as a government fund or foundation) or contractor towards a project's running costs. They are the cost of supporting the work, above the direct costs of actually doing the work. Many donors allow NGOs to charge a fixed overhead, sometimes called a 'Negotiated Indirect Cost Recovery Agreement'. For conservation NGOs, this is typically between 15% and 30% of the direct project costs but it can be as high as 60% for US universities and 100% for UK universities. Commonly in the consultancy world, donors do not permit such management fees; they specify that office-related costs are incorporated into an overhead applied to a salary (for example, salary costs x 40%). However, this system is not well suited to international NGOs: in the developing world, it creates an incentive (indeed a need) for involving higher-paid expatriate staff on projects, because they generate more money in overheads for the organisation than lower-paid local staff.

There are also 'matching funds'. Most donors ask that applicants contribute towards a project's funding – either as cash or in kind – or demonstrate that they have found others willing to do so. Donors typically specify an expected minimum contribution. Donors do this partly because they want to know that the applicant is serious about the project and partly because they themselves want to run efficiently and to maximise the impact their funding makes. Larger donors like to report the amount of funds their donation has 'leveraged'; some take this a step further and create 'challenge grants', to encourage others to give. In other words, a donor organisation will say 'We will give this amount if others come in and give the same'. In 2001, the philanthropist Robert W. Wilson set the Wildlife Conservation Society a US$20 million 'challenge grant' to support their work in ten wilderness landscapes around the world. The precise amounts given from the grant each year were calculated on the basis of how much 'new money' the organisation had raised in the preceding year. If, after paying core costs, a conservation organisation has a surplus of unrestricted funds, this may be put towards matching funds, but only the richest conservation organisations can do this.

Project managers need to be creative in finding matching funds: one approach is to secure smaller grants to finance certain activities and then combine these into a bigger grant proposal. Another is to ask a private business to contribute some unpaid work to the project, which can then be presented in a grant proposal. In 2005, the leading market research company, Nielson, supported a project studying the trade in wild birds in Indonesia by including researchers' questions in its bi-monthly survey of urban households. The commercial value of this support amounted to several thousand pounds and was included as matching funds in a (successful) grant application. It also ticked another box in the donor's eyes: an innovative delivery partnership. Volunteers' work is also becoming included in matching funds and ticks other buzz-words such as 'participation'. Imagine a local conservation group, running an urban educational reserve and looking for a grant to provide holiday educational activities for children. If they have a group of volunteers each contributing 20 hours a week organising and assisting with activities, they could multiply this by a reasonable hourly rate and include it as matching funds on their application.

Sources of unrestricted funding

Fee-paying members and subscribers – a guaranteed, and relatively stable, source of unrestricted funds – are key to the success of many conservation groups. They are a group which can be asked for additional donations for specific campaigns, be sold goods and services and be a valuable organisational asset for policy.

Even so, not all conservation NGOs are membership organisations – and some quite large conservation organisations have small memberships – because there are considerable efficiencies of scale, both at the lower end of the scale (fewer than 3000 members) and at the higher end, with memberships of 50,000 and above. There are many small conservation societies and clubs that finance their operations from a fee-paying membership of just a few hundred or thousands, such as The British Cactus and Succulent Society and the Oriental Bird Club. These clubs are run by volunteers; their memberships need only limited maintenance. Members tend to find and stay with such clubs because of their passion for the cause or subject, so a two to three thousand-strong membership might require just eight to ten hours a week of administration.

Expanding specialist-size membership into mass membership takes a lot more money. As a membership grows beyond 5,000, the tasks become too much for volunteers and it becomes necessary to employ someone and invest in more sophisticated database and communication technology. More significantly, building up membership means going out and attracting members and offering something that appeals to a wider (and possibly less discriminating) audience. This might be an attractive magazine or opportunities to visit nature reserves, participate in campaigns and meet other members. Such inducements have obvious financial consequences, although these vary considerably with the size of the organisation. A membership magazine with a circulation of hundreds of thousands might pay for itself from advertising revenue, whereas one serving a membership of ten thousand may consume a significant proportion of the membership dues received. Similarly, planning and designing an initiative to engage members in a campaign to lobby the government will cost the same (apart from postage) whether the membership is a thousand or a hundred thousand. From a raw financial perspective, memberships start becoming significant sources of income when they go above 50,000.

Beyond the basic work of making sure that existing members receive their publications and get a nice letter when they pay their subscriptions or reminder when their subscription has lapsed, larger memberships give the organisation the opportunity for statistical analyses. Sophisticated profiling of the membership – what issues they are interested in, which projects they prefer to support, how much money they give, how old they are and so on – yields valuable information. With this information, organisations can better focus their messages and target certain members for particular fundraising appeals. Such analyses also strengthen the hands of those responsible for selling advertising space in the organisation's publications.

However, large memberships can also be something of a double-edged sword. As memberships increase in size, they are likely to contain greater proportions of casual supporters; people who join on a whim but change their priorities when renewal time comes round. NGOs do everything they can to avoid this, such as trying to persuade new members to pay their subscriptions by annual direct-debit, but even so, 10% to 15% of large memberships are likely to lapse each year. Quite apart from the financial implications, a declining membership makes everyone edgy both because of the financial implications and the symbolic value of a large membership. To deal with this threat, membership recruitment is becoming increasingly strategic. A common piece of analysis is to link membership and national census data through postal (zip) codes. This enables the NGO to identify areas that fit the demographic of their existing membership but where they currently have few members – fertile ground for recruitment drives. This kind of analysis can also provide insights into members' wider interests and media preferences, which can be used to design better advertising strategies.

In the UK, the RSPB uses postal code analysis to identify areas where recruitment drives are most likely to succeed. One area identified as having a lower than predicted membership was the 'Mersey Belt', the conurbations around Liverpool, Manchester and Leeds, which cut across the north of England.

RSPB research suggested that people would agree to join on or after their third positive contact with the organisation – a 'three strikes and you're in' strategy. So, the RSPB started moving into the lives of the northern English professional classes. They developed the educational potential of their reserves close to urban areas in the Mersey Belt, ran a national 'garden bird-watch' with the *Today* programme on BBC Radio 4, and broadcast live footage of nesting peregrine falcons on big screens in many city centres. People visiting the RSPB's *Aren't Birds Brilliant?* activities in places such as Malham Cove, a famous and magnificent nature monument in the Yorkshire Dales, are welcomed by RSPB volunteers and, after watching nesting peregrine falcons through their telescopes, are politely asked 'are you a member of the RSPB?' Who could possibly refuse?

Many people are willing and able to leave legacies to conservation organisations. Legacies ('planned giving', as it is called in the US), give organisations a steady and substantial source of unrestricted funds that allows them to invest in development and growth. They also offer supporters the opportunity to make the decision to give now and pay later. In many countries legacies are exempt from death duties: in the UK, up to £312,000 can be left to friends or relatives tax-free, after which an inheritance tax of 40% is levied. Many people with estates in excess of this figure choose to leave the residue to favourite charities. Conservation NGOs do not have to work too hard to secure legacies once they have an established membership and a public profile. The main techniques are polite, non-pushy advertisements in members' magazines and informed advice on how to make a will. Some American organisations have taken this one step further, offering legacy planning tools on their websites. Gifts of land or property are rare in Europe but much more common in America; NGOs such as Nature Conservancy will accept land either as reserves if it meets their science-based conservation criteria or as 'trade lands', which they can sell. In the US, 'conservation easements' are a further incentive to give land to conservation.

Some worry that funding from legacies may decline due to factors outside NGOs' control: Only time will tell. The decline of final salary pension schemes, greater longevity and mobility and increasing requests from children for help with house buying are all biting into capital. More recently, the downward turn in the global economy, caused by the world-wide 'credit crunch' could also hit this important funding stream hard. The US$20 million gift to the Wildlife Conservation Society we mentioned earlier was very large, but in the USA, gifts of over a million dollars are not that unusual and gifts over US$100,000 are almost common. High net-worth individuals (HNWIs) are a major source of finance for American conservation NGOs but hardly feature in their European counterparts' income. Partly, this is cultural: amassing great wealth is part of the American dream, enabled and encouraged by a historically generous tax regime, a vibrant economy and a deeply entrepreneurial spirit. Along with these privileges comes the unwritten responsibility to give something back – to causes of your own choice. Europe's Socialist tradition and entrenched class divisions have created cultures where wealth is taxed more deeply and with a greater expectation that the state will deliver public benefits, such as conservation.

NGO trustees in America and Europe also have very different cultures. In America, being a trustee is a social accomplishment, which marks someone as a prominent citizen and one of the élite. Most trustees of smaller organisations come from the same city or state: trusteeship therefore opens access to élite social networks. Trustees both actively help their NGO to identify and build relationships with other HNWIs and may themselves make substantial contributions; hosting dinners to introduce wealthy friends to conservationists, arranging for them to visit field sites and generally trying anything in their power to

encourage donations. Nearly every famous American conservationist has a story of taking a rich heiress or business magnate to
an amazing natural landscape and, as they gazed out across a
magnificent panorama, popping the question: 'will you buy this
place for eternity?' The reply has frequently been a resounding
'Yes!' The prosaic reality is more probably that such moments
will have been carefully engineered, over many months, by a
team of trustees, the NGO's staff and fundraisers. This is not
cynical manipulation: donors genuinely want to make the gift
and truly value their new friendships and the opportunity to
move into interesting social circles. They may also become
staunch supporters and future trustees of the NGOs. Gala
dinners are another important part of HNWI networks. They
bring a conservation organisation's community together –
employees, partners, high society and aspirant élite – to celebrate
and recognise the achievements of the organisation and its staff.

European, and especially British conservation organisations,
are seemingly neither very adept nor very comfortable with this
sort of fundraising. It is not that gala dinners and their like
cannot work in Europe. In 2007 a small conservation charity,
Elephant Family, organised a very successful event in London
that generated over £500,000. However, trustees of British
conservation NGOs are chosen more for their ability to watch
over the organisation and the entrée they provide into establishment networks rather than their links to private money.

The Internet is a powerful new tool for fundraising. It makes
it easy for supporters to give online to an appeal or purchase
'virtual gifts', such as a hectare of rainforest. Search engine
technologies make it possible for organisations to reach new
supporters by increasing the likelihood that a website will appear
when a conservation-related search term is entered. The US
President Barack Obama's election campaign set a new standard
in Internet fundraising, gathering 87% per cent of its funds from
online giving: 90% of the donations were under US$100. The

campaign did it by integrating social networking sites, such as Facebook, Myspace and Twitter, with its website. Harnessing the power of peer pressure, through strategies that encourage supporters to network and prompt each other to give, is likely to become a vital aspect of future conservation fundraising.

Foundations and trusts are private organisations, created to hold and manage assets used for charitable purposes. They vary enormously in size and scope and have different portfolios, but all are governed by groups of trustees. The original founders of some trusts (such as the MacArthur Foundation) have since died and their foundations are now managed by trustees and professional staff. In other cases (such as the Gordon and Betty Moore Foundation), the founders are still alive and take an active interest in the foundations' activities; yet others are family foundations, where control is handed from one generation to the next. Some foundations like to invest in big schemes, such as the Moore Foundation's support for Conservation Internationals' Hotspots campaign; some support emerging talent and leadership, such as the Whitley Fund for Nature, which makes ten awards of £30,000 a year to up-and-coming conservation leaders, mostly from developing countries. But the majority of foundations fund continuing project work.

Depending on the size of the trust, and the amount to be dispersed each year, some trustees employ staff to manage their grants. The Chicago-based MacArthur Foundation has assets of approximately US$6 billion and employs 180 staff. This foundation makes grants of US$225 million a year to projects on global security, human development, the environment and conservation. Foundation funding differs markedly between the US and Europe. In 2005/6, a report by the Environmental Funders' Network – an informal network of trusts, foundations and individuals that makes grants on environmental and conservation issues – put the total amount invested in the UK by 176 environment-related foundations at £33.6 million, with an average grant size of just under £19,000; five years earlier, in the US, the Gordon and Betty Moore Foundation made a US$261 million grant commitment to Conservation International.

Getting a grant from a foundation is not easy. There is a lot of competition; success depends on who is applying, the quality of the idea and the seriousness of the cause. Some foundations offer a relatively transparent and open application process; for others, applications are invited – which means getting to know one of the trustees or a grant manager. As with most areas of conservation funding, relationships are vital and many foundations prefer to fund organisations with which they have long-term relationships. In America, where the biggest conservation organisations have their headquarters and the biggest foundations are based, programme managers and foundation grant managers meet to discuss ideas and shared interests and to work up projects. Some European NGOs with international programmes maintain American offices so they can develop these relationships and be eligible to receive funds from US foundations.

For many developed countries, grants from foreign governments are a major source of conservation finance. In 2005/6, the UK government made grants estimated at £396 million for biodiversity conservation, whereas the figure for NGOs was estimated at £156 million. Internationally, the signing of the Convention on Biological Diversity in the early 1990s led to an enormous increase in government funding. Such funding falls into two categories: bilateral and multi-lateral. Bilateral funds have been used for the establishment of national parks, the preparation of national conservation strategies and even the construction of tourist facilities. Bilateral funding was, originally, government to government funding and typically followed the classic model of development aid, in which one country provides funds and technical assistance to the government conservation agency of a less-developed country to help it achieve a specific outcome. However, in the 1990s, many governments began providing funds directly to international conservation NGOs that had partnership agreements with a government agency. For some aid bodies, this became the preferred route for donations.

In multilateral funding, a group of countries puts money into a fund, which is then dispersed to countries in need of financial support. The biggest multilateral fund for conservation is the Global Environment Facility (GEF); the funding mechanism for the Convention on Biological Diversity. The Convention recognises that the benefits of biodiversity conservation are global but that developing countries in the tropics, with great biodiversity, bear most of the responsibility (and costs) for protecting it. After the Rio conference in 1992, richer Western countries contributed over US$1 billion to the GEF and have since replenished it with a similar amount. Two intergovernmental agencies, the World Bank and UNDP, manage and disperse these funds. Initially, these new funds for biodiversity conservation went directly to the governments of developing countries. One of the largest single grants (of US$32 million) was for an integrated conservation and development project in the Kerinci–Seblat National Park in Indonesia. Many intergovernmental conservation grants were linked to development projects being financed by the World Bank in the same country and region and managed by teams from the World Bank and senior bureaucrats of the host country government. The work was carried out by government departments, with large components contracted out to specialist consultancies and – to a lesser extent – conservation NGOs.

In response to lobbying from influential conservation NGOs, in 1996 the GEF incorporated a mechanism, the medium-sized grant, through which they could directly apply for funds of up to US$1million. This was a massive change for conservation

NGOs in developing countries, which had previously patched together their funding from numerous small grants (often less than US$30,000) and perhaps a couple of large foundation grants of US$150–200,000. The GEF created the possibility that NGOs could increase the scale of activities and reduce the overall number of donors in a programme. Securing access to these new funds meant the NGOs had to modify the way they worked. Organisations such as the World Bank, USAID, DANIDA (Denmark) and DFID (UK) all have similar, clear and quite bureaucratic procedures for assessing the merits of grant applications, dispersing funds, accounting for spending and monitoring the progress and impact of a project. Very few will fund 'pure' conservation projects. Since the Millennium Development Goals were agreed, which set the alleviation of poverty as the major goal of intergovernmental aid, conservation organisations seeking to secure funding have had to show how a project can support delivery of these goals. Understanding what is needed and building donors' trust and belief in an organisation's capacity to meet those needs is a critical part of the funding process; both things that well-established, Western conservation organisations are in a better position to do than their Southern counterparts.

Attitudes to corporate fundraising differ dramatically. At one end of the spectrum, some NGOs (for example Friends of the Earth) resolutely refuse to take money from corporations because part of their *raison d'être* is to hold those corporations accountable for the environmental damage they cause. At the other end, the US-based Nature Conservancy has some 1,900 corporate sponsors; in 2002 they donated a total of US$225 million. Although fundraisers often jest that 'the only problem with tainted money is there t'aint enough of it!', most conservation groups have criteria for the type of company from which they will accept funding and for the basis on which they will

PROJECT MANAGERS: BUREAUCRATS OF THE CONSERVATION WORLD

Project managers are the main cog in the system of conservation practice; the interface between government and foundation donors and the teams working in the field. Their work – mostly desk-based – is a combination of contract management, technical support and networking. It is one of the most common jobs in modern conservation and most professional conservationists must have good project management skills.

European and American conservation organisations enter into delivery contracts with major donors based on a logical framework, universally known as a 'logframe'. This specifies the project's objectives, its budget (broken down into expenditure categories) and its main components and activities, with indicators to verify that the work has been carried out. The project manager's task is to agree a detailed work and financial plan with the team implementing the activities, organise the funds and specialist support, monitor whether activities and expenditure proceed according to plan and edit the team's reports to the donor. In the complex world of conservation, things rarely go to plan; another of the project manager's responsibilities is to agree changes to workplans and the logframe with the donor.

The project manager must also ensure that the project's activities are technically well informed and reflect current best practice. Many project managers are highly qualified and provide direct technical support, bringing in additional expertise as required. They are also the advocate for the project within the organisation. The larger NGOs are becoming ever more strategic and hard-nosed in their decisions about their investments: key to a project manager's success is ensuring that a project aligns with the organisation's strategy, is seen as important by senior managers and has a high profile in the organisation's publicity. This sounds very bureaucratic – and it is. Those who get funds from governmental agencies must become a bit like them.

enter into a financial relationship. Companies are becoming more strategic and view funding as a partnership; the conservation organisation may even become involved in company policy. The Hong Kong and Shanghai Bank (HSBC) donated £35 million to Earthwatch so that the bank's staff could join conservation expeditions and become attuned to the need for corporate social and environmental responsibility. More cynical commentators suggest that such funding may be part of a company's risk management strategy; a close association with a conservation or environmental NGO (especially a powerful one) reduces the risk of attacks from the media or other environmental groups.

Whatever the companies' motivations, significant corporate funding comes through the development and maintenance of close relationships between conservationist groups and companies. This means more than simple cash. For conservationists, such relationships provide access to business know-how and networks and often result in valuable work-in-kind contributions. The wildlife trade-focused American NGO, WildAid, has a long-standing and mutually beneficial relationship with the global advertising agency, J. Walter Thompson.

Finding new financial sources

The costs of conservation are rising all the time. This is partly because the threats to wildlife are becoming greater but also because many conservation organisations are getting bigger and slicker, which brings ever-increasing salary bills. NGOs can try to squeeze a bit more from their members, or a new conservation-friendly foundation might appear, but neither of these significantly adds to the overall sum available. And the big push of the late 1980s and early 1990s to get governments to contribute more to biodiversity conservation now seems to be waning, as government funds are redirected to other priorities such as poverty alleviation and climate change. Leading conservation groups, such as the Nature Conservancy, WWF and Conservation International, have engaged experts to develop ways that either make it more attractive for people to donate or release new money that can be used to finance conservation. Here we will introduce five such devices, two old and three newer and more speculative.

Conservation easements were one of the first devices specifically designed to support conservation. They are mostly an American tool but are starting to gain ground in Canada, Latin America and Australia. Easements involve a legal agreement between a landowner and a land trust or government agency to preserve the land for its conservation value. They are essentially a way of increasing the area of land available for wildlife without having to raise funds or lobby a government. Furthermore, they empower landowners to protect their land from future development: if the land is sold the 'easements' remain binding. Tax benefits for gifts of conservation easements date back to 1977 but the system really took off after the US government introduced the Uniform Conservation Easement Act in 1981. Easements are rooted in the idea, enshrined in US law, that individual rights with respect to the use of land can be separated from the 'bundle' of rights represented by the ownership of the land. A landowner can give up certain rights, such as the right to further development or sub-division, while retaining other rights, such as restricting access. Conservation NGOs work with government agencies to enable landowners to donate rights to a government conservation agency or approved land trust and receive tax benefits in return. So as long as they meet the tax requirements, the reduction in market value attributable to a donated easement may be considered a charitable donation that makes the landowner eligible for a federal income tax deduction and estate tax benefit. Conservation easements are a wonderfully cost-effective way of maintaining wildlife-rich habitats and landscape beauty, because the land does not need to be bought but only those rights which, if exercised, would reduce the land's conservation value. Money does not need to be tied up in land purchase, which frees limited funds for other projects. Conservation easements are now promoted, held and managed by over 1500 land trusts across the USA. Land trusts monitor their properties permanently, to ensure the agreed easement restrictions are not violated. These restrictions are invariably locally focused and based on conserving the natural character of a particular landscape or area.

Conservation easements have been a hugely successful device. Of the 15.4 million acres protected by the Nature Conservancy in the United States, more than two million are made up of conservation easements. The Nature Conservancy helped pioneer the easement concept and, along with the Land Trusts Alliance, was influential in enshrining it in law and helping government agencies and land trusts build their expertise. Nowadays, the network of land trusts, the Nature Conservancy, and others, are an influential voice behind policy and legislation relating to conservation easements and promote interest in easements as a tool for estate planning and management.

Debt-for-nature swaps were an inspired idea of the econo-mists of Conservation International, WWF and the Nature Conservancy; Conservation International completed its first swap in 1987. Their underlying principle is very simple. As we know from the high-profile campaigns of Bono and other celebrities, developing countries owe Western governments and banks billions of dollars in loans. This 'debt burden' is a major obstacle to development and sound environmental management, because a substantial proportion of the funds of that country is spent on repaying the loans. What might be less commonly known (although the 'credit crunch' has brought it to light), is that 'debt' is traded in secondary markets and can be purchased at a price significantly lower than its face value. In its simplest form, a conservation organisation can use its funds to buy this sovereign debt and then to negotiate a deal with the debtor government to redeem it. This might be as simple as restricting development around a protected area but more normally involves the debtor country setting up a local currency trust fund to finance an agreed portfolio of conservation projects. The conservation group negotiates a redemption value equal to or higher than the sum they bought the debt for, to provide more local currency to conservation groups than would come from a straight donation. Alternatively, instead of buying the debt, the conservation organisation may facilitate an exchange or transaction between two governments; both the Nature Conservancy and Conservation International broker deals between the US Treasury and its indebted nations. In 2006, they organised the largest-ever debt-for-nature swap, under the US Tropical Forest Conservation Act. In this deal, the United States agreed to 'forgive' US$26 million of debt owed to it by Costa Rica and in return, Costa Rica promised to spend the equivalent in local currency in conserving tropical forests in six areas. The sites were chosen from a blueprint that the Nature Conservancy helped to create for Costa Rica

To conservation organisations, the value of debt-for-nature swaps goes well beyond their financial value. They attract positive media attention and portray the organisation concerned as entrepreneurial and economically sophisticated. They do however involve intense negotiations between commercial banks and finance ministers, powerful groups and individuals with which conservation organisations have previously had little contact. Conservation NGOs often have a great say in how funds are dispersed and how conservation frameworks are employed. This helps conservation groups extend and embed their philosophies in developing regions.

The Holy Grail of environmental economists is to create a market for ecosystem services: the fresh air, water and fisheries vital for economic stability and growth but rarely included in economic models. In the language of economists, they are 'externalities', ingredients of production processes but which producers and consumers get for free or pay very little for. People think they get air, water, erosion control, nutrients and more for free because they are difficult to value and even more difficult to build into systems of economic exchange. Much effort has focused on getting users to pay for the valuable ecosystem services of forests, such as watershed protection and carbon storage and three approaches are emerging. The first, Voluntary Contractual Arrangements, usually operate at a local scale: for example, a hydropower company in Costa Rica pays the Montverde Conservation League, which owns most of the forest catchment, to protect forests so as to maintain steady stream flows and low sediment loads. The second, Public Payment Schemes, involve governments asking companies for a fee for ecosystems services and then indentifying the key areas at which the income is targeted: for example, the Chinese Forest Ecological Benefit Compensation Scheme involves levying an tax on water and tourism businesses operating in scenic areas and using this money to finance forest protection and restoration.

The third approach – the one that grabs headlines because of climate change – is trading in ecosystem services: a government or group of governments sets a limit on the amount of ecological services that can be used – it issues quotas that can be traded. In carbon trading, this is a cap on how much a company can emit. Sulphur dioxide, salinity and nutrient trading schemes also exist but carbon trading is the focus of current action and has entered public consciousness though a plethora of carbon footprint calculators and ideas for how to reduce individual and corporate carbon emissions. A key concept is the notion of 'offsets' or 'offsetting': because carbon dioxide has no geographic boundaries, companies and individuals that cannot reduce their emissions can 'offset' them by buying into a new initiative that captures carbon or stops it being released. This creates a market for 'credits', which are measured in tonnes of carbon emitted or sequestered. The great hope is that carbon trading will create financial incentives for not cutting down forests, planting new ones or restoring degraded ones. There are two markets for carbon credits: the compliance market and the voluntary market. The cost of credits in the voluntary market is cheaper, because they are not subject to the rigorous UN validation of credits traded under the Clean Development Mechanism (CDM), a flagship intergovernment scheme. This market is popular with individuals and companies that want to offset their emissions voluntarily. Because few people have sufficient expertise in offsetting, specialist companies are springing up to fill the gap. Travellers who offset their travel with the UK-based company Climate Care put their money into green energy projects operated by local companies which sell their carbon credits to a broker, who sells them to Climate Care, which sells them on again.

Much time and money is currently expended on efforts to bring forest conservation into the compliance market. At present, only reforestation projects are allowed under the CDM, although conservationists want the conservation and sustainable management of existing forests to be eligible when the present round of post-Kyoto negations is concluded in 2009. Conservation lobbyists and policy-makers are aiming to build credibility for a mechanism tabled by the Council of Rainforest Nations, led by Papua New Guinea and Brazil: Reduced Emissions from Deforestation and Degradation (REDD). Forest loss and damage contributes around 20% to greenhouse gas emissions; the REDD mechanism would enable countries to receive payments if they reduce deforestation. However, there are many challenging issues: first, how to know whether a forest would remain if the scheme were not enacted. Second, how to set national and regional baselines of existing forest cover and deforestation rates against which carbon emission or sequestration rates can be measured. Third, is leakage – the possibility that even if a forest patch is protected, loggers or plantation companies might simply cut down another, so there is no net carbon gain. Fourth, how can we be assured that the forest is both in the state claimed and will remain that way. If all this isn't difficult enough, there is currently very little data on how much carbon dioxide different types of forest release when they are cut down and how much is sequestered by different forests growing under different conditions. The response of conservation organisations and scientists has been impressive. Certification experts at WWF are working on a 'green carbon standard' to tackle assurance issues and university researchers are conducting fundamental research on the basis of standard measures of carbon per cubic metre of timber by timber type, region and growth phases.

The potential market for REDD is between US$2 billion and US$31 billion, a great deal when one considers that the total overseas development assistance available for forest conservation is currently around US$1.5 billion. Many people are sceptical that the market forces that have destroyed forests can now be used to save them but conservation organisations are investing their best brain power in the hope that they can. The latest idea to come from this free-market philosophy is 'biodiversity offsets' in which mining companies and their like ensure that their operations cause no net loss of biodiversity by paying for conservation elsewhere.

7

Conservation's critics

Most of us would agree that conservation is 'a good thing' and that it is important to protect the Earth's endangered habitats and species. But – perhaps surprisingly – there are both major criticisms of conservation from outside and some worrying internal rifts and debates among conservationists. The conservation movement has been criticised for, among other things, keeping rural people poor, displacing indigenous people, appropriating native lands, perpetuating inequality, engaging in corporate 'greenwash' and spending too much of their donations on executive salaries and perks. Furthermore, in the eyes of some commentators, this has been done in a quest to deliver a vision of nature that originates from (and largely benefits) people in affluent Western societies.

One of the biggest debates is about how much impact conservation can justifiably have on people's lives and their economic opportunities, especially in the developing world. Generally, conserving nature and the environment has widespread political and public support and is opposed by those whose interest is in making profits. However, some conservation practices (particularly setting aside large tracts of land for wildlife – and the tourism for the better-off that goes with this) are increasingly criticised by academics, NGOs and journalists concerned with social justice, alleviation of poverty and development. Their arguments hold weight, because nearly all extensive areas of 'natural' land (other than Antarctica) have been exploited to a greater or lesser degree by humans. Indeed, it is often the communities that are most dependent on natural resources who live in the most remote areas; communities that are the least able to adjust if displaced in the name of conservation.

Fortress conservation

'Fortress conservation' describes the practice of excluding local people from protected areas. Tracts of natural, or semi-natural, land are often important both to conservationists and to local people but problems can arise because each group and its supporters have very different starting points. In the past, conservationists have tended to think about and designate protected areas using criteria that largely ignore the needs of the human inhabitants. They promote a rational, planned management, with biodiversity and ecosystem services protection as its main objectives. Local communities, when they have been considered at all, are a means to an end: potential partners, enrolled in the conservation effort through employment, community development grants or nature-related livelihood activities. The conservationists' agenda has typically strengthened the power of the state by extending rationalised, centralised land use management into remote areas and producing international funding. In contrast, the desires of indigenous peoples and local communities almost always begin with the securing of legal rights to 'their' land and resources. Understandably, they want the authority to govern their land and make their own decisions on how to use it. Their agenda is political: a desire for autonomy from the state means that the state is unlikely to generate significant revenues through taxes or investment.

Sociologists, anthropologists, geographers and others who are interested in these issues sometimes complain that conservation agencies do not have clear policies to deal with voluntary or involuntary displacement of people from newly protected areas. Such policies are needed; there is considerable evidence that displaced people are more likely to become ill, die early, lose their home, job, access to resources or become marginalised and socially dislocated. The conservation movement's record is not particularly good when compared to other concerns – for example dam and road-building – that may mean people need to be resettled; governments and others have developed strong policies and organisational protocols to deal with such dislocations. Perhaps significantly, some of the most withering criticism has come from academics closely associated with the World Bank. They are particularly concerned about issues arising from forced evictions following the rapid expansion of protected areas in Africa during the 1990s. They argue that protection imposes and reinforces an idealised vision of 'wild' Africa while portraying the conservation of biodiversity and ecosystem services as an overarching public good. Protection and conservation arguments are then used to legitimise the removal of local populations. Recognising the risks to local communities of such dislocations, the World Bank has developed policy standards for involuntary displacement that have been widely adopted.

'Conservation refugees', displaced in their thousands from protected areas, are starting to become the subject of articles in the popular, not just specialist, media. And there is increasing interest in the 'economic displacement' that occurs when people are excluded from their traditional hunting and fishing grounds, forests and agricultural land. The removal of people's rights to continue doing what they have always done can cause great cultural and personal disruption and hardship. There is also growing evidence to show that displaced people are frequently neither adequately nor properly compensated. Poor rural people are bearing the major costs of conservation and the main beneficiaries appear to be Western middle and upper classes.

Conservation stands accused of taking a free – or at least a cheap – ride at the expense of the poor. Are such serious accusations justifiable? Conservationists clearly recognise the principle that displaced people need to be properly reimbursed: at the World Conservation Parks Congress held in Durban in 2003, it was recommended that where negative social, cultural and economic effects occur as a result of the creation or management of protected areas, the affected communities should be fairly and fully compensated. However, critics argue that the big conservation organisations have still neither translated this recommendation into formal resettlement policies nor put such policies into effective practice. It has also been suggested that there is no real pressure on them to do so, because most displacements from newly protected areas happen in remote areas, far from public scrutiny. Pressed on this issue, conservationists often respond with positive words or suggest that displacement is a matter for the government; that they are partners, funders and technical advisors, not the authorities responsible. This line of defence, even if true, is somewhat disingenuous, because conservation organisations are very much part of the international development sector and members of the multi-organisation alliances that determine the fate of rural peoples.

The core of the criticism of fortress conservation comes from academics studying the relationship between colonialism and African environments. Their key insight is the recognition that conservation activities protect and sustain not just wildlife and its habitat but also particular ways of envisioning nature. Our images of African wildlife and landscapes – vast herds of wildebeest sweeping across the Serengeti, meerkat clans scampering around the bush, lions gathered around a kill – are, essentially, carefully framed and staged portrayals. In the BBC and National Geographic versions of Africa and on the websites of conservation groups, the everyday life of the people who also live in those landscapes is scarcely represented. When the local people are there, they are depicted as noble (or chic) savage, poacher or loyal helper and companion (or enemy) of the white conservationist, scientist and film-maker. These conservationists, scientists and film-makers are people with a vocation, living uncertain, exciting, interesting – and sometimes arduous – lives, in close proximity to nature. Unlike indigenous Africans, they have a lifestyle many in the West dream of. Connecting with these dreams is pleasurable and those with the money, time and connections can live them for a time on safari holidays, hunting trips or as volunteers on a project, watching television, reading books or – increasingly – following and contributing to blogs or logging on to live webcasts.

Seen from the perspective of conservation, this Africa (or Latin America, or Asia) is a simulacrum – a copy of something that no longer exists and perhaps never really did. It is richly populated with visions and practices from the books, magazine articles and public lectures of the élite conservationists of the colonial era. The images are all there – the game drive, noble nature, hunting with the camera, the native tracker and helper, the lodges, the sun-downers, the camp-fire reflections, the escape from the stress and vice of modern urban living. An experience, its critics say, that is as much about reliving the past and experiencing the colonial relations of privilege as about understanding the present. Critics of conservation are not necessarily against such representations: these versions of the past, romanticised in films like *Out of Africa* and *White Mischief* and in the staged accounts of African wildlife on the Discovery Channel, are popular everywhere and part of our global cultural heritage. Moreover, for an Africa suffering from the ravages of HIV/AIDS, widespread poverty, armed conflict and despotic leaders, they represent one of the few positive portrayals of the continent in the Western mind (not to mention the tourism revenues they generate). Where critics take issue is with their negative consequences for the traditional and poor people of

Africa and the perceived complicity of 'big conservation' in sustaining the situation.

An influential 2004 article, 'A Challenge to Conservationists', written by Mac Chapin and published in *World-Watch* magazine, extended these arguments to criticise the relationship between the 'big three' conservation NGOs (Conservation International, WWF and the Nature Conservancy) and indigenous peoples. His argument has three strands: first, that the rapid growth in income, geographic reach and financial muscle of these organisations has led them to believe that they are legitimate authorities in their own right. Second, that they have appropriated the 'indigenous' for fundraising purposes but not fully integrated indigenous people's agendas. Finally, that these NGOs design internationally appealing conservation strategies, such as biodiversity hotspots and Global200 eco-regions, and then argue that they are the only organisations that can manage them – setting up a closed shop.

Although the amount of revenue available for biodiversity conservation has declined by almost half since its peak in the late 1990s, the funds channelled through the 'big three' have increased, both relatively and absolutely. In 2002, it was estimated that more than half the approximately US$1.5 billion available for conservation in less-developed countries was generated by and channelled through WWF, the Nature Conservancy and Conservation International. A more recent study (based on 2006 figures) put the total expenditure of 278 conservation organisations operating in Africa at US$200 million. More than 50% of this total was spent by the top five organisations and 65% by the top ten. In Africa, the 'big five' are WWF (by far), Conservation International, the Wildlife Conservation Society, the African Wildlife Foundation and the Peace Parks Foundation. With the exception of WWF, they are all American organisations. Money does not equate directly to power; what matters is the network of relationships that are built up through spending money. Several of the larger conservation organisations direct the flow of donor aid by dispersing smaller grants to local NGOs. The justification is that this widespread practice is cost-effective for donors and that the big conservation NGOs are well placed to assess the capacities of local NGOs and monitor their progress.

Between 2004 and 2005, Conservation International provided grants to 161 NGOs in Africa and 153 NGOs were supported by their Critical Ecosystem Partnership fund. They also fund university scientists, research institutes and private individuals. However, the criticism is that, to secure grants, local organisations must be seen to endorse Conservation International's view of conservation. Another accusation is that channelling donor money into less-developed countries attracts those countries' most talented young professionals to the big conservation NGOs and their local clients, because the salaries and career prospects are better. This is not wrong, but it could stifle the emergence of independent, and culturally specific, conservation movements. Spotting and assimilating local talent into the global conservation movement arguably strengthens international conservation but to the detriment of indigenous groups. In both national and international policy, the days of white Western men articulating a conservation vision for less-developed countries are passing into history. A new generation of educated and articulate Ugandans, Colombians, Indians, Brazilians and others now represents international and local conservation and is putting forward its own case. In contrast, indigenous groups risk appearing backward and concerned solely with their own interests, rather than national or global concerns.

Conservation is important to Western governments: their political credibility comes from how many millions of dollars, pounds or Euros they disburse. Their citizens expect that a percentage of their taxes is spent on environment-related inter-national development but they are perhaps less interested in how well this is spent and who benefits from the aid. Agencies talk of their 'burn rate' – the rate at which they spend their money in delivering aid. Of course, they have procedures and frameworks to work within but the big NGOs help them to spend the aid money on time. Big conservation NGOs – organisations that ooze professionalism and respectability – have people who can merge the languages of development and conservation, who can guide the cash over and around bureaucratic hurdles and who can justify the flows of money through visions of cutting-edge science. Staff working for international conservation organisations become very close to senior staff working for international aid agencies and to senior staff working in government ministries. Career paths have begun to join, as high fliers move easily between government organisations and NGOs. These people are part of the inter-state polity and have the authority to steer developing countries in how they govern their natural resources and the people whose livelihoods depend on those

"*Relax, we're from Conservation, Inc.*"

Figure 15 A critical cartoon of 'big' conservation
"*Relax, we're from Conservation, Inc.*" © *William Bramhal, reproduced with permission of the artist*

resources. The growing role of big conservation organisations in international policy has led to accusations that they are assuming the authority and attitudes of international agencies. Organisations such as WWF, the Nature Conservancy and Conservation International can use the power that comes from portraying themselves as intergovernmental organisations to some audiences and as civil society organisations to others, yet without taking on the responsibilities typically associated with such roles. The big NGOs are accountable neither to political masters, public constituencies nor markets. This gives them an 'edge' that governments, commercial organisations and the majority of other (smaller) NGOs in the world do not have.

Chapin's second strand deals specifically with the relationship between conservation NGOs and indigenous groups. He argues that indigenous groups feel let down, used and increasingly threatened by some conservation organisations. The rift can be traced back to the 1989 appeal by the Coordinating Body of Indigenous Organizations of the Amazon Basin (COICA) for environmental groups to form an alliance to 'defend our Amazon homeland' and include indigenous peoples in their vision of the Amazonian biosphere. This struck a powerful chord with American conservation NGOs: the Amazon was (and still is) threatened by ill-conceived development projects, cattle ranching, soya production, unregulated logging and mining and more and the public interest in and support for indigenous people was growing through publicity campaigns by groups such as Survival International and films such as John Boorman's *The Emerald Forest*. The first Amazon summit meeting between indigenous peoples and environmentalists was attended by delegates from indigenous communities in Peru, Bolivia, Ecuador, Colombia and Brazil and members of leading American conservation NGOs, WWF, Conservation International, the Wildlife Conservation Society, the Rainforest Alliance, the Sierra Club and the environmental groups

Greenpeace and Friends of the Earth. Everyone signed the 'Declaration of Iquitos': an alliance of indigenous peoples and environmentalists for an Amazonia for humanity. At the fourth World Congress on National Parks and Protected Areas, held in Caracas in 1996, the IUCN and WWF produced a report, *Principles and Guidelines on Indigenous and Traditional Peoples and Protected Areas*. The main problem it identified was that when international conservation NGOs and indigenous peoples worked together, the projects tended to be designed by the NGO, the execution tended to be paternalistic and naïve and the input of the indigenous peoples limited. The worldviews of Western biologists and project managers and indigenous representatives were worlds apart. In these circumstances, both sides are frustrated and very few real partnerships can be developed. What irked Chapin (and others) was that the big conservation organisations used the rhetoric of indigenous involvement in their conversations with donors and their public fundraising campaigns and yet, when it came to providing a platform for indigenous views, kept noticeably quiet. The NGOs wanted to be a-political and not upset any of the hundreds of corporate partners who contribute to their revenues.

The final point of Chapin's criticism is that because conservation NGOs help define large-scale natural resource planning and also argue that only they have the capacity to manage these areas, they are drifting towards becoming de facto planning and management authorities for the landscapes that indigenous people claim as theirs. What is more, the science that conservation organisations employ is often not very compatible with – and might even be in stark contrast to – indigenous peoples' vision for their environment. Some indigenous leaders are becoming increasingly concerned by big landscape conservation schemes. Schemes such as Conservation International's hotspots, WWF's Global200 and the Wildlife Conservation Society's 'living landscapes' influence how donations flow, what commercial operations may and may not take an interest in the land and how government officials and others might interact with local communities. However, despite their undeniable interest, it is difficult for indigenous groups to find out about these schemes before they are launched, let alone contribute to them or understand their design. Furthermore, the international conservation NGOs seem to have divided the global conservation territory among themselves: in central and south America, Conservation International has major interests in Suriname and Guyana, the Nature Conservancy operates in Nicaragua, while the Wildlife Conservation Society controls the gateway to the Bolivian Chaco. In Sumatra, Indonesia, the Wildlife Conservation Society is the conduit for American donation flows to the south, WWF to the middle and Conservation International to Aceh, in the north of the island. For indigenous groups, the thinking and strategy of big conservation NGOs may be even less transparent and obvious than that of big businesses.

As if all this were not enough, journalists in America have started to publish hard-hitting exposés of the big American conservation NGOs, accusing them of 'getting into bed' with big business or worse, starting to act like big businesses. In 2001, the Pulitzer Prize-winning environmental reporter, Tom Knudson, published a series of reports, 'Environment Inc.' in the *Sacramento Bee*. Two years later, the *Washington Post* ran its influential 'Big Green' series, which exposed some questionable land deals made by the Nature Conservancy, involving the selling of ecologically sensitive land to its trustees at discount prices. One of the latest criticisms comes in Christine MacDonald's book, *Green, Inc.*, which extends and reiterates the key themes of many of these exposés. MacDonald's argument is that, by providing paid 'greenwash' for businesses, conservation organisations cancel out their good work. Essentially, her argument challenges the prevailing logic of 'big conservation'; that engaging with big business is a pragmatic and necessary compromise in the quest for green global capitalism and that helping and encouraging markets, corporations and investors to adopt environmentally strong standards will deliver more conservation benefits than will a few isolated interventions. Scepticism about conservation's association with industry has focused on tactics and organisational self-interest. MacDonald points out that Greenpeace's confrontational 'day of protest' at the European offices of Unilever caused the company to stop buying palm oil from Indonesia. In contrast, WWF and the Nature Conservancy appear to be engaging with palm oil interests on projects that are, in effect, planned deforestation. The second argument is that by accepting funds from mining, power and plantation companies, conservation NGOs lose their ability to act as watchdogs and worse, may (intentionally or not) become corporate apologists. There have also been accusations that much of this corporate money goes into giving six-figure salaries, creating plush offices and paying for top conservation executives' fact-finding trips to exotic destinations.

Conservation's pragmatic response

Leading conservationists agree with their critics about the importance of debating the issues they raise, but argue that those critics often present a misleading, monochromatic portrayal of conservation action; criticising specifics while ignoring the bigger picture. It is not a choice between doing conservation well or doing it badly: it is about trying to find ways of changing that succeed in the messy and political real world. Whether or not Unilever buys palm oil from Indonesia is incidental to the survival of patches of Sumatra's hugely diverse lowland forests. The oil palm boom means that concessions are being granted to companies to convert the remaining forest (most of which has already been logged) into plantations. The forest is going to be cleared whatever happens. Environmentalists cannot hope to save eighty per cent of what is left: realistically, there may only be an opportunity to save ten to twenty per cent of whatever is left in five to ten years' time. The only way to do even this is to work with companies willing to protect some forest within their concession.

'Fortress conservation', and its extension to the relationship between conservation organisations and indigenous peoples, is particularly troubling, because it could drive an unnecessary wedge between conservationists and local communities. This would be a tragedy; both groups are struggling against the same challenges – globalisation, corrupt governance and irresponsible corporate activities. Some conservationists note that critics have assumed the role of talking for poor, marginalised and indigenous peoples without providing any justification for it. This leads some to suspect that some critics see conservation as an easy way to give their particular (and often highly political) opinions and perspectives a high profile and decent credibility. (A similar argument suggests that prominent criticisms of conservation earn journalists awards.) Conservationists do not attempt to deny that indigenous peoples are displaced but, increasingly, argue for a more subtle understanding of the issue. For example, many reserves were settled after they were established; settlers sometimes own other lands and by settling are simply staking a claim to what they perceive as 'empty' land. In some cases, under the banner of conservation, governments have displaced people for political reasons, such as strengthening territorial claims or disrupting communities where political dissidents have traditionally found refuge. And compromises may simply not work: a conservation organisation's objective of conserving mammal populations may be just incompatible with the maintenance of traditional hunting practices. In these situations, a stark choice has to be made between humans and nature. The community of nations has agreed that conserving the world's natural heritage is a public good but that in such projects (as in any public project – airport, dam, mine or national park) some people will inevitably lose out. Conservation organisations are just one of a number of groups whose responsibility it is to ensure that when resettlement is unavoidable it is done fairly and

BACK TO THE FUTURE: LIVING WITH PREDATORS

Finding ways for people and predators to co-exist is far better than separating humans and nature and avoids displacement and animosity. In areas where large predators such as cheetahs, jaguars, snow leopards, wolves and so on live, the idea of farmers and predators living together harmoniously seems preposterous. Livestock owners everywhere have always sought to eradicate predators from their land, decimating populations and strengthening the case for uninhabited reserves.

Many compensation schemes attempt to dissuade farmers from trapping, poisoning or shooting predators but they have had mixed results, not least because they involve farmers in frustrating bureaucracy. An American cheetah expert, Laurie Marker, learnt that in most parts of the world which once had abundant wildlife, livestock owners kept fierce dogs but in South Africa, the dogs kept by herders (perhaps understandably) feared predators. Moreover, herders tended to move their stock away from danger, which merely triggered a cheetah's instinct to stalk and give chase.

Marker researched dog breeds and came across the Anatolian Shepherd, a huge dog, traditionally used by Turkish shepherds, that stands its ground and protects the herd. Marker's Cheetah Conservation Foundation bred Anatolian Shepherds and distributed them to farmers in Namibia: livestock losses dropped to zero and cheetah numbers are increased. Conservationists plan similar livestock guard-dog programmes using Anatolian Shepherd to help farmers feel more at ease with landscapes inhabited by wolves (United States), snow leopards (Nepal), jaguars (Brazil) and lynx (Switzerland).

appropriately. Singling conservationists out for special criticism is like holding water engineers accountable for displacements linked to dam-building. Conservationists argue that the key issue is not so much what they do but how they do it. All is not perfect but the major conservation bodies point to a transformation in conservation that has been going on since the 1970s. This is characterised as 'community-based conservation', an approach that actively engages local communities in the design and implementation of conservation projects.

The traditionalist critique

Ironically, a second major criticism of modern conservation comes from within the ranks of conservation itself. Some (typically older) conservationists have argued that in moving towards community-based conservation, the conservation movement risks undermining its core purpose of protecting species and wild places. They suggest that conservation has, to all intents and purposes, become another type of rural development, operating in and around natural areas, and that this change in emphasis has engaged conservation in development activities outside its core competencies, distracted attention from the saving of critically endangered species and forced some conservation organisations to be less than honest with their supporters. In short, other agencies are better placed to help rural people and conservationists should focus on being a voice and a force for nature and wild places.

Many of these critics' worries revolve around the concept of community and whether or not economic incentives actually change long-term behaviours. There is a powerful argument that much community-based conservation is based on a rather idealised view of traditional village governance that only rarely exists; the assumption that communities are homogenous, self-governing entities that can make and uphold decisions in their long-term self-interest. In reality, communities are complex and heterogeneous, and decision-making is coloured by minority interests and family ties. Many rural villages in developing countries are best seen as multiple communities, with overlapping interests; the receptiveness of these different communities to conservation initiatives varies widely. Some of these communities are reluctant, or unable, to defend their resources from outsiders and if they try, there may be nasty conflict.

There are also justifiable worries that conservation groups are simply not very good at rural development work; they lack the training, networks, expertise, secure long-term funds and organisational structures. Many conservation NGOs work in partnership with, or sub-contract to, local NGOs but the cost of rural development is still high in terms of fundraising, contract management and reporting. Community conservation involves working with communities to reduce their impact on nature by developing alternative, more sustainable, ways of living but the evidence that improving livelihoods leads to better conservation is rather limited and contradictory. Commonly, a community

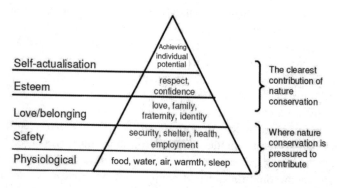

Figure 16 Conservation's contribution to Maslow's hierarchy of human needs

may adopt new ways of living yet maintain its old extractive practices, or a flourishing village may attract immigrants, putting new pressure on natural resources. And there is always the risk that if a new, more compelling proposition (for example, logging or growing oil palm) comes along, villagers might switch their allegiances.

Many of the traditional conservationists' criticisms are differences in opinion about the fundamental philosophy and purpose of conservation. Traditionalists identify with the idea that conservation is about building, and reinforcing, a less human–centred ethic, which recognises both that other species have a right to exist and that human societies need wild places too. They argue that this message is implicit in the communication and fundraising activities of many conservation NGOs and that conservation should keep true to this ideal, even if this means smaller organisations and less access to international development funds and high-level policy making. A more human-centred way of looking at this is to think of conservation in terms of the American psychologist, Abraham Maslow's, Hierarchy of Human Needs (Figure 16). At the bottom of his hierarchy are physiological needs (eating, breathing, sleep), followed by the need for security (of health, of employment, of family) and so on up the pyramid. Conservation's contribution lies in the potential of nature to help people achieve the higher levels: self-actualisation, esteem and belonging. According to this argument, there are better ways of delivering basic human needs than by using nature.

What can we make of the criticisms and debates circulating through conservation? Many of the problems of modern conservation stem from the compromises that organisations must make to keep people employed and attract and retain the talented people they need. Some of these compromises are justifiable and inevitable – conservation organisations must make hard decisions and cannot please everyone. However, problems have arisen because of the weak governance and accountability systems that characterise some conservation organisations. One way to overcome these criticisms is for the members of conservation groups to be a little more questioning, and a little less trusting, of the organisations they support.

8

Twenty-first-century conservation

Conservation was one of the most successful cultural movements of the twentieth century. Perhaps its most remarkable achievement was the setting-aside of vast areas of the globe for nature: some 12% of the Earth's land mass. However, the success of conservation cannot be measured simply in acres or dollars: even more important has been the changing of people's attitudes. Nature conservation, once a radical idea that cut against the grain of society, has become a mainstream interest. Conservation organisations have played a central role in this change. Since the 1970s, some organisations have transformed themselves into major international organisations, with global reach and influence. What does their future hold? Will conservation in 2020 or 2050 be broadly similar to today or will climate change – the biggest of all current environmental anxieties – radically change its direction and influence, as fear of pollution did in the 1960s?

The Nobel Prize-winning physicist, Nils Bohr, famously quipped: 'Prediction is very difficult, especially if it's about the future'. One prediction that seems clear to us is that a transformation of conservation is not only likely but inevitable, perhaps even imminent, given the accelerating rate of social and environmental change. Change seems certain; as society changes and new knowledge about humans' impact on the planet becomes widespread, our conservation values, goals and ideals must alter. Just as we might be horrified to know that our grandmothers lusted after a fur coat made from the skin of a rare cat, our grandchildren might find our consumption of bottled water from throwaway plastic bottles equally abhorrent. This chapter outlines eight predictions for conservation in the twenty-first century. We offer them as pointers to and points of interest for debate, reflection and hope. Some are based on the extrapolation of current trends in global conservation; others are pure speculation on our part.

Prediction 1: climate change continues to dominate the conservation agenda

We have not said that much about climate change. But we assume you are aware of the issues and some of the predicted consequences for society and environment. The most recent prediction of the Intergovernmental Panel on Climate Change (IPCC) is that global temperatures could rise by between 1.1 and 6.4 °C (2.0 and 11.5 °F) during the twenty-first century. As if this were not bad enough, the scientific consensus is that warming, and sea level rise, will continue even if (an enormous 'if') the global community manages to stabilise carbon dioxide emissions. In other words, without some form of unforeseen technological 'fix', the Earth will be forced to undergo an unprecedented period of change.

Although climate scientists have developed some robust methods to predict future climates, it is much harder to predict the consequences of environmental change for species and ecosystems. The main technique conservation scientists use is to assess and map the 'climate envelope' in which a species currently lives. Climate change will move the boundaries of this 'envelope' and if a species cannot move with them, they may be set on the road to extinction. Some mountain animals require cold conditions: global warming may mean that the climate envelope of some species will move so far uphill that their habitats will disappear off the top. But climate change will create both winners and losers. Some previously rare species may find that their potential geographic range has expanded dramatically, especially those plants and animals currently at the edge of their range. A 2003 study predicted that national parks in the USA will eventually have an average of 50% more mammal species, due to northward migration.

It is likely that the climate change winners will be far outnumbered by the losers. Huge efforts are under way to identify the likely losers and so concentrate conservation efforts on the most vulnerable species and habitats. As yet, there is little consensus on how best to help such species. Some well-publicised (and heavily criticised) estimates suggest that up to a million species might eventually be driven into extinction by climate change. These are big, scary numbers which have, understandably, drawn the attention of policy-makers and politicians worldwide. The responses of the conservation movement

Figure 17 A Dutch 'greenway' linking two fragmentary habitats (photo © rijkswaterstaat/joop van Houdt Fotografie)

to the threat of global climate change have varied but generally involve improving linkages (corridors, greenways and so on) between protected areas, so that threatened species can move to more suitable habitats if they need to. This is part of the rationale behind international schemes, such as the Pan-European Ecological Network (PEEN) and the Meso-American corridor, whose aims are to link together protected areas. Ideally, there would be sufficient links between protected areas to allow endangered species to move with the changing climate. Unfortunately, intensive development of the countryside may mean this isn't possible and other solutions, such as translocations and reintroductions, may be needed.

Climate change has had some, perhaps unintended, consequences for the conservation movement, because it is often easier to deal with a potential threat than a messy real-world problem. Climate change has drawn attention away from traditional species and habitat protection projects, even though habitat loss, fragmentation, invasions and unsustainable exploitation currently pose huge threats to the natural world. Many of the best minds in conservation are occupied lobbying governments to avert the worst impact of climate change, rather than tackling immediate problems. Whether this focus on climate change is justifiable or whether the conservation movement has taken its eye off the ball will become apparent in the first few decades of the twenty-first century; whichever turns out to be true, climate change is set to dominate the conservation agenda in the foreseeable future.

We do not know exactly how the natural world will be transformed by climate change, despite scientists' best efforts. What we can predict is that the conservation movement will react to changing conditions and re-align to meet new challenges with new solutions and innovative policies. Conservationists may try to store genetic material, so that species can be brought back into existence when the climate stabilises.

Or new visions of conservation may arise, which reject traditional notions of naturalness and focus on building ecosystems
that serve human needs or feed human imaginations.

Prediction 2: China emerges as a major force in global conservation

Just as carbon dioxide emissions are pushing the Earth into a
period of accelerated climatic change, so the phenomenal
growth of the Chinese economy – and China's drive to find the
resources to fuel it – is driving a rapid and fundamental change
in global geopolitics. China does not do development 'aid' in
the Western sense but its massive state companies negotiate joint
ventures with governments in Africa, Asia and Latin America
and are willing to do business with regimes of questionable
reputation – regimes generally avoided by American and
European companies. Chinese companies often enter into deals
under which they create infrastructure in return for resources or
a stake in resource extraction companies. Chinese companies are
rebuilding the railways of the oil-rich Nigeria and Democratic
Republic of Congo, pumping US$8 billion into road and rail
infrastructure and bringing mines back into production. This is
far from charitable: in return, the Chinese have gained a 68%
stake in a Congolese mining company with rights to two large
copper and cobalt mines.

Such Chinese investment will undoubtedly boost the
economies of these poor and unstable countries but improved
access to remote regions is also likely to hasten the demise of
their wildlife and forests. Ironically, growing environmental
awareness within China may be accelerating the plunder of trees
from overseas, because as the Chinese government responds to
internal and international pressure to introduce forest protection
and restoration polices, it must look elsewhere for its timber. In

2003 scientists from Beijing's Forestry University estimated that China's demand for imported wood for furniture-making, construction and paper production will grow by at least a third between 2005 and 2015. The US Environmental Investigation Agency believes China to be world's largest buyer of illegal timber and its major investments in the transport infrastructure of the rainforest countries of Africa and south-east Asia can only hasten the clearing of the remaining forests. China is also a major consumer of wildlife products; new roads will open up once-remote areas to hunters and trappers. The prospects for tropical forests and wildlife look bleak and the last big areas of relatively untouched rainforest in the Congo are likely to be utterly transformed by the middle of the twenty-first century.

Since the eighteenth century, conservation has piggy-backed on Western economic and political colonial power. This era of superiority is now at an end. Developing countries can now choose between Western and Eastern development partners. Chinese investment comes with fewer environmental and social strings attached: East Asian cultures put very different values on wildlife and nature. The Chinese river dolphin (the baiji), the last member of a unique family of mammals, became extinct in the Yangtze river in 2007, despite years of decline and a clear understanding of the forces driving it towards extinction. It is hard to imagine this would have been allowed to happen if the baiji had lived in the Mississippi or the Rhine.

However, despite the doom and gloom, there are reasons to be cautiously optimistic about Chinese conservation. The considerable power the Chinese government has over its people means it has an enormous ability to engineer social change, as illustrated by the well-publicised 'one child per family' policy that its government imposed in the 1970s in response to the problem of population growth. If such power were used to promote environmental values and behaviours, it could create remarkable change in a relatively short time. And there are signs that China is developing an indigenous conservation movement. Increasing numbers of students are educated at Western universities, and international conservation NGOs are slowly gaining a foothold in a country with a notorious suspicion of foreigners.

Prediction 3: conservation becomes increasingly industry-led

Bizarrely, considering their past reputation for environmental destruction, the major resource industries – mining, oil and gas, timber and plantation companies – may become key players in environmental protection. Currently, most people believe governments, NGOs, wealthy individuals, and sometimes traditional communities, own and manage protected areas. In future, conservationists might have to add trans-national companies to the mix and accord them the access to policy and funding presently reserved for non-profit organisations.

Companies are starting to incorporate conservation in their business model: eighteen of the hundred companies listed in Business in the Community's 2006 *Corporate Responsibility Index* said biodiversity was an area in which companies should be assessed. This reflects the accumulating evidence that businesses that take corporate social responsibility seriously gain significant financial and market benefits. Many resource companies own vast areas of natural habitat and their operations (such as mining and oil extraction) do not necessarily require them to clear all, or even much of their land. Protecting this land for conservation can enhance security as well as the company's image. Plantation companies must clear land but many are contracted to leave some timber uncut. These companies realise that developing strategies for identifying and protecting high-conservation value forest opens opportunities to develop new markets for sustainable cash crops. The companies are also able to secure lower-cost investment and gain a market advantage, because they are perceived as 'greener' than their competitors. Companies may also be able to trade the carbon credits tied up in uncleared forests. In Chapter 6, we described the RSPB's bold initiative to buy and manage 100,000 hectares of threatened lowland Sumatra rainforest, at a cost of several million pounds. A little further to the north, a major pulp company, which owns massive areas of forest, is planning to protect a further 200,000 hectares by implementing a mosaic planting scheme that will maintain high conservation values and carbon assets, as well as producing the timber needed to supply the mill.

In developing countries, some industries may be better at delivering conservation than either governments or NGOs. There are at least six areas in which business has an advantage over conservation NGOs (Table 5). If comparative benchmarking of corporate, government and NGO management of conservation reserves were undertaken, it could well be that corporations would come out on top. More likely, major resource extraction industries and conservation NGOs may form land or reserve management partnerships in which the company runs the reserve and the NGO takes care of the science, policy and marketing.

Whatever the precise outcome of various initiatives, we expect the development of a very different relationship between the international conservation establishment and industry. The 'people-power' environmentalism of the 1970s brought about a relationship often of antagonism and suspicion but this attitude has softened in the last two decades, resulting in numerous NGO–business partnerships. In the near future, we expect conservation NGOs will stop criticising corporations who clear forests and work with them to plan deforestation and design multiple-use landscapes in which natural forest blocks and corridors fit with production. This is not a perfect situation but would be a considerable improvement on the current default scenario; complete destruction.

Table 5 Reasons why industry can deliver better site-based conservation in less-developed countries

Reason	Explanation
Time scale	Resource-based companies plan and budget their operations over decades whereas conservation NGOs are financed by short-term grants from donors who rarely fund beyond five years.
Land tenure	Industries are major land owners or lease holders in less developed countries which brings more political power.
Resources	Few NGOs have the financial, logistic or human resources necessary to engage in long-term management of substantial areas of land in developing countries. In contrast, successful resource-extraction businesses have by definition had to develop the technical and operational expertise to manage land and incorporate this into their business structures, planning and ethos.
Human Resource Management	Strong social and environmental credentials help a business attract talented and creative employees. Because the core business of NGOs is conservation this activity brings no competitive advantage in terms of human resources.
Accountability	Industries report publicly on their performance and a number of structures exist to hold them to account. No such pressure is exerted on government and non-government conservation groups.
Governance	Companies operating in remote areas are major employers, which means they can wield far more influence locally than a conservation group can.

Prediction 4: the extinction debt will be paid

Studies of oceanic islands tell us that the bigger an island, the more species it can hold. And as the size of an island reduces, some species are squeezed out. For oceanic islands, this reduction normally takes millions of years, as the island slowly erodes into the sea, but it happens much more quickly when newly created 'islands' of forest find themselves surrounded by agricultural land. More species are lost as climatic conditions within the remaining habitat change beyond the ability of its organisms to cope. This reduction of diversity does not happen immediately; habitats all over the world now owe a significant 'extinction debt'. In other words, many nature reserves and remaining fragments of habitat contain species that have travelled a long way down the road to extinction. These doomed, but not yet extinct, species are termed *Acheronian*, after the souls who, with insufficient funds to pay the ferryman, were doomed to wander the banks of the River Acheron for a hundred years before they were allowed to cross into Hades, the land of the dead.

We have been lucky. There have been very few high-profile species extinctions since the 1960s. But many species are barely hanging on and it can only be a matter of time before the world experiences extinctions on a par with those of the passenger pigeon or the thylacine. One of the groups most at risk is the primates, because many species are reliant on having good-quality rainforest to live in and are hunted as bushmeat. Currently, eighteen species of primates in Indochina have populations of fewer than 250 individuals. A rash of high-profile extinctions could shake public trust in conservation and might be interpreted as evidence that conservation organisations and governments are not working effectively.

Perhaps the extinction of the mountain gorilla, the orang-utan or the Asian elephant might galvanise the next generation of conservationists and lead to the birth of new and more successful conservation organisations and movements. These large, charismatic species are unlikely to be allowed to become extinct in the wild: they are simply too important. When their situation becomes critical, huge resources will be thrown in their direction. It is most likely that the extinction debt will be paid by numerous, less well-known, species of invertebrates, amphibians and reptiles – species that most people know little about and, arguably, care even less. Such extinctions will not go completely unrecorded or uncommented but are unlikely to force a change in global attitudes to conservation.

Prediction 5: conservation of the oceans comes to the fore

Our focus in this book has very much been on conservation of terrestrial species and habitats, which reflects the emphasis of conservation during the twentieth century. But we predict that conservation of the oceans will emerge as an exciting and compelling new cause in the twenty-first century.

The oceans are currently in a terrible state. In his excellent, if depressing, book *The Unnatural History of the Seas*, Callum Roberts describes the once-teeming life of our oceans and the devastating impact of centuries of commercial fishing and hunting on its abundance. 'Fishing down the food chain' captures the true seriousness of the situation: commercial fleets with ever bigger boats and ever more powerful technology have driven several species to commercial extinction – and some close to biological extinction. Fishermen have thus turned their attention to smaller and smaller species of upper ocean fish and, more worrying still, to deep sea species, which reproduce and grow at much slower rates. A startling example is the orange roughy, a deep sea fish that can live for 150 years; it does not even reach sexual maturity until it is 20 to 30 years old. Over-fishing has caused many populations of this incredible fish to crash and, due to its long life cycle, there are no prospects for a quick recovery.

Marine conservation's relatively low profile during the twentieth century is partly explained by the political power of the commercial fishing lobby and partly because beyond 200 miles from the shore the oceans are a commons, outside national or supra-national control. However, the biggest problem is, arguably, that the changes in the marine environment have been largely invisible to all but a few. Most of us think of the oceans as a flat expanse, sometimes blue and sparkling; sometimes rough and cold. Seas teeming with fish, whales and turtles are a lost memory for contemporary society. Until very recently, it was only possible to get an occasional insight into the variety of life in the seas and the horrendous impacts of commercial fishing, offshore development and waste disposal on marine ecosystems. Destructive practices have continued in the oceans that would never have been tolerated on land.

David Attenborough's *The Blue Planet,* first shown on the BBC in 2001, was instrumental in bringing the wonders of the ocean to a mass audience. However, one of the most exciting developments in conservation is the 'back to the future' Planet Ocean Initiative (www.protectplanetocean.org). This initiative replicates two of the key insights of the nineteenth-century conservationists: first, that major change comes not through organisations but through informal and eclectic networks of individuals at the cutting edge of science, politics, business and technology; and second, that conservation approaches with a simple, no-argument logic, work best where governance insti-tutions are weak. Planet Ocean was initiated by Dan Laffoley, a British government marine specialist from Natural England and marine vice-chair of the IUCN World Commission on Protected Areas. Professor Laffoley teamed up with the deep-ocean explorer, Sylvia Earl, who was awarded the 2009 Technology, Entertainment and Design (TED) Prize. This unique award chooses one outstanding person from each of these fields of human endeavour and grants them their wish to change the world. They receive US$100,000 in cash but, more importantly, the prize gives them access to the extraordinary TED social network. Earl's wish was: 'I wish you would use all the means at your disposal – films! expeditions! the web! more! – to ignite public support for a global network of marine protected areas, hope spots large enough to save and restore the ocean, the blue heart of the planet'.

The platform for this wish is an innovative partnership with one of the biggest IT companies in the world, Google, to put the ocean floor into Google Earth (http://earth.google.com). Version 5 of Google Earth, launched in February 2009, includes a detailed bathymetric map of the ocean floor; new Internet technologies allow users to 'dive' under the water and explore the seafloor in three dimensions. A range of partners, including National Geographic, the US Navy and the IUCN has contributed information and the ocean bed is filled with 'pop-up' windows providing videos, pictures and text on species, sites and threats. It is an amazing development and far more than 'edutainment'; it is a state-of-the-art conservation advocacy tool, with massive potential. Conservationists and researchers can use the information to analyse and pinpoint threats or as a base on which to overlay new information about endangered species and populations. Field workers can link video reports of local issues and activities through file-sharing sites, such as YouTube. If you read this book after April 2010, Disney will have launched its extraordinary new film, *Oceans*, while National Geographic television will be amazing people with an animal's-eye view of the seas, produced by new cameras mounted on the shoulders of sea creatures. The network is bringing the oceans into the public mind, stimulating the wider consciousness and creating a demand for action. Together, conservationists can demonstrate to decision-makers just how serious are the threats to the world's oceans and just how pitiful the global response has been.

The ultimate goal is to urge and press governments to designate more and larger marine protected areas (MPAs). MPAs have many similarities to the wildlife refuges and sanctuaries designated in the early twentieth century: places for wildlife, governed by one simple rule – no exploitation – with no exceptions. Where this rule has been implemented and enforced, the results have been spectacular: the response of the marine community to protection can be startling and rapid. A study published in 2000 by scientists from Auckland University of the strictly protected Tawharanui Marine Park in northern New Zealand demonstrated that legally sized specimens of the commercially important spiny lobster became eleven times more abundant after fishing was completely prohibited in 1983. And within ten years of banning fishing in part of a small Caribbean marine reserve around the island of Saba in the Netherlands Antilles, the overall biomass (the combined weight of all individuals) of commercially important fish species had increased by 60%. Even more staggeringly, the biomass of one group, the predatory snappers, had increased by 220%.

Together with predicting that conservation will fully embrace the challenge of protecting the marine environment, we also envisage that conservationists will continue to break out of their narrow organisational compartments and operate through networks that link a range of diverse professions. Conservation will embrace and drive new developments in media and technology and this technology will bring the individual citizen back into mainstream conservation and gener-ate new insights into the work of conservationists.

Prediction 6: return of the wild

A number of new strands of conservation thinking and practice are starting to coalesce as 're-wilding': the reintroduction of extinct species, normally large herbivores and predators, into natural areas to restore their ecological function. The ground-breaking Dutch project to re-create Europe's large herbivore assembly (mentioned in Chapter 1) challenges established ideas of conservation and may point the way to new, complementary conservation strategies. The architect of the project is Frans Vera, an ecologist with the Dutch nature conservation agency, Staatsbosbeheer. He became interested in the effects of grazing on vegetation after observing the effects of grazing by moulting goose flocks which congregated every year on an abandoned polder. His observations led him to challenge the established view that Europe was once covered with forest; in his hypothesis he argues that, in at least some areas, herbivores controlled the forest structure. The Dutch government allowed Vera and his colleagues to set up a public experiment of his ideas at the 6000-hectare Oostvaarderplassen reserve. In the mid-1980s, Vera's group introduced red, fallow and roe deer, Konic ponies and Heck cattle to the reserve. Konics are a very old breed, thought to be very close to Europe's extinct horses, while Heck cattle are a breed developed in the 1920s by the Heck brothers, of Germany, who cross-bred the oldest breeds of cattle they could find to create an animal that resembled the last known European species of wild cow, the auroch, which became extinct in 1627.

A visit to Oostvaarderplassen is a surreal and conceptually challenging experience. It is rather like looking across a cold Serengeti; herds of cattle, horses and deer intersperse with flocks of geese and shorebirds that occasionally rise in vast clouds as an eagle drifts into view. After the initial spectacle has sunk in, a number of fascinating questions confront the conservationist. Should we view the cattle and horses as domestic species used as a management tool to deliver conservation targets or as conservation targets in their own right? Did the auroch and tarpan (the Eurasian wild horse) actually become extinct? Did humans transform aurochs and tarpan into cattle and horses and is the Oostvaarderplassen the crucible of their rebirth? Is the reintroduction of large herbivores and letting nature take its course sensible? The experience of Oostvaarderplassen and other sites in Holland where they are introducing 'naturalistic grazing' suggests that while the abundance of some species may increase, the overall diversity of species may decline. Is this good or bad? Could it suggest that re-wilding is an approach for ex-agricultural land rather than for existing reserves?

Reconstituting former large mammal communities is not confined to Holland. The 'Pleistocene Park' project, in Russia, aims to return the taiga to the tundra steppes through the creation of grasslands and the introduction of bison, musk ox,

Figure 18 The Oostvaaderplassen: letting nature take its course (photo © Vincent Wigbels)

Yakutian horse, hares and marmots. The reintroduction of predators is planned, once herbivore populations have become firmly established. In East Anglia (in the UK), the Great Fens Project has a long-term and phased strategy to re-wet 3,700 hectares of farmland to connect the Holme Fen and Woodwalton Fen National Nature Reserves.

We suspect that re-wilding projects will expand significantly both in number and popularity. While orchids, frogs, bitterns and the like appeal to the traditions of natural history that persist in the white middle class, large mammals fascinate a broad cross-section of Europe's increasingly multicultural society. The synchronised birth of Heck calves or the rutting of stags are natural spectacles with a universal appeal. Re-wilding projects can bring nature to the forefront of public debate. Letting the wild-acting cattle starve to death at Oostvaarderplassen outraged Dutch animal welfare organisations so much that they took Vera and his organisation to court. The debate focused on notions of cruelty; in particular why it is considered cruel to allow natural winter starvation and yet not cruel to separate social animals from their mothers at an early age. If we are to renegotiate society's relationship with nature to meet the rapidly changing environmental and social circumstances of the twenty-first century, such debates are critical.

Scientifically, re-wilding epitomises the 'functionalist' approach to conservation; giving priority to managing and restoring ecological processes. This contrasts with the 'compositionalist' approach, the dominant conservation paradigm of the twentieth century, which emphasises the conservation and management of species and species assemblies. Faced with the prospect of climate change, many conservation scientists argue that it will be impossible to retain the existing composition of species both in reserves and the wider landscape, and that we have no choice but to focus on restoring and strengthening ecological processes so that natural systems can adapt.

Prediction 7: an end to extinction

We suspect that public interest in re-wilding projects and re-introducing species will grow during the first half of the twenty-first century. The reintroduction of species such as the beaver, lynx, Californian condor or wolf is an antidote to the doom-laden stories of destruction and extinction that seem to dominate the headlines. But will advances in genetic technology and conservation combine to bring species back from the dead?

The science journalist Henry Nicholls has prepared a revival recipe for extinct species: take well-preserved DNA, several billion DNA building blocks, a suitable surrogate mother and some highly advanced technology. In 1960, we could not have imagined being able to clone a sheep, so such ideas may not be as preposterous as they first appear. The Australian Natural History Museum, in Sydney, has attempted to clone the extinct thylacine (Tasmanian tiger). According to Nicholls, the woolly rhinoceros is a good candidate for resurrection. Like the mammoth, there are plenty of specimens of this animal preserved in permafrost and it has close living relatives. The dodo would be more difficult: pigeons could possible take on the role of surrogate parents but only a few dodo bones and skin fragments exist, and these have produced hopelessly poor-quality DNA. The giant ground sloth, which became extinct 8,000 years ago, falls in the 'extremely unlikely' category. Several specimens have been found bearing hair, which is an excellent source of DNA. The difficulty would be finding a suitable surrogate for this six metre-long, four-tonne whopper!

Some leading geneticists think such projects are a waste of time and that cloning a species from ancient DNA is, and will always be, impossible. Conservation organisations are also cool on the idea, arguing that the prospect of a 'technofix' will distract public attention from the more urgent need to save existing species and undermine the imperative for action that follows from the knowledge that extinction is forever. Nevertheless, public enthusiasm for 'Jurassic Park-style' science, coupled with advances in cloning techniques suggests to us that more teams of bioscientists will be attracted by the technical challenges, the scope for publicity and funding and the fact that it is such an intriguing idea.

While it is impossible to know whether re-wilding of extinct species will ever really happen, we'd be willing to place a (very) small wager that tourists of the late twenty-first century will be able to head off to the Russian steppes for photo safaris with the big five; woolly rhinoceros, musk ox, auroch, Siberian tiger and bison. Re-wilding, reintroductions and reversals of extinction will be an increasing source of hope, inspiration and controversy.

Prediction 8: conservation is linked to health and well-being

The late nineteenth-century pioneers of conservation had little trouble making the connection between the protection of nature and humans' well-being. Town-dwellers of this time routinely suffered from respiratory diseases, such as tuberculosis, that had no simple cure. They turned to nature – country walks, taking the sea air – to relieve their conditions. City living is still unhealthy; today's urban ailments are obesity, stress and anxiety. These diseases are quite different from their nineteenth-century counterparts but their symptoms can also be alleviated through regular contact with nature, such as visiting a 'wildlife spa' (otherwise known as a nature reserve).

Medical science is beginning to re-embrace the idea that regular contact with nature should be an integral part of health care. At present, there has been very little research done and so little evidence is available to back up this widening of health policy. And, of course, the powerful pharmaceutical lobby has a keen interest in maintaining the status quo. We predict this will slowly change as the social and economic costs of dealing with contemporary urban diseases rise and as citizens increasingly take responsibility for their health. The breakthrough will come when conservationists start describing 'wellness' as an ecosystem service and a gifted economist is able to quantify its value. We need to see some rigorous scientific studies into whether there is a relationship between visits to natural areas and a reduction in obesity, stress, anxiety or other medical conditions. It seems likely that the medical research councils will commission such research. If the link is made, and if it is accepted by politicians and the medical establishment, 'recreation-based conservation' will be born.

End point

Our discussions have largely been about current trends in conservation and how these are likely to extrapolate into the first half of the twenty-first century. The further one looks into the future, the harder it is to accurately predict what might happen. However, there are four very good reasons to think that the practice and focus of conservation at the end of this century will be radically different to the way it is today.

First, climate change will cause huge shifts in the composition and structure of ecosystems, necessitating a major re-think of conservation strategy and focus. Second, technology will continue to develop, dramatically increasing the kinds of interventions available to conservationists. Third, the world population will change – present predictions show it increasing until about 2060–2070 and then declining. Conservation will be radically different in a time of population loss – an indication of how different can presently be seen in northern and eastern

Europe, where a decline in population has gone hand-in-hand with reforestation. Finally, social values will continue to change – and not necessarily favourably to conservation.

It is tempting to speculate that the need to move countless species in response to climate change, combined with mass human migrations, may change human attitudes to non-native species. Our grandchildren's generation may be far more likely to ask what *can* live here, rather than what *did* live here. Or perhaps, future societies will create complex mosaics of reserves, spanning everything from Jurassic Park-style re-creations of pre-industrial habitats to fully-functioning exotic ecosystems.

You may have picked up this book to read because you are thinking of pursuing a career in conservation, volunteering your time, donating some money or wondering about a cause you would like to get involved with. Our message is: *please do* but please do it with an open and questioning mind. Conservation is entering a critical, dynamic and exciting phase; it needs innovative ideas, original perspectives, fresh enthusiasms, new kinds of commitment and people able and willing to ask hard and insightful questions and offer imaginative and inspiring visions. If, as most experts suggest, humanity is entering a period of accelerated social and environmental change, conservation and conservationists, as well as the species and habitats they seek to save, must change.

In our view, the best way to adapt is to connect – unite with, and become part of, the forces that are shaping the future. Since the middle of the twentieth century, conservation maintained a distinct identity, which, in some ways, has kept it conservative and lacking self-awareness. Relatively stable, if limited, funding from subscribers, foundations and governments has enabled ten or so organisations to dominate the market and create stable networks in which they operate in a steady, low-risk way. A shake-up may be needed to help conservation connect and adapt and the pressure for such a change must come from people outside, as well as inside, conservation groups.

The human resources, talent, commitment and expertise available to conservation are better now than any time in its history. As people in the privileged position of teaching a Masters course, we are continually amazed and heartened by the intellect, knowledge, commitment of so many young (and not so young) people around the world ready to devote themselves to a career in conservation. A multitude of professional people from all walks of life is willing to volunteer its time; influential people are willing to listen to conservationists and an ever greater number of organisations are willing to recruit staff with conservation or environmental-related expertise. The challenge is to channel this potential into new and exciting projects that will define the conservation agenda of the twenty-first century.

Further reading

Adams, W.M. (2004). *Against extinction: The past and future of conservation*. Earthscan, London

Borgerhoff Mulder, M. & Coppolillo, P. (2005). *Conservation: Linking Ecology, Economics and Culture*. Princetown University Press, NJ

Callicott, J.B. (1994). *Earth's Insights. A multicultural survey of ecological ethics from the Mediterranean Basin to the Australian Outback*. University of California Press, Berkeley, CA

Gaston, K. & Spicer, J. (2003). *Biodiversity: An Introduction*. Wiley-Blackwell, Oxford

Ladle, R.J. (Ed.) (2008). *Critical Concepts in the Environment: Biodiversity and Conservation*. Volumes 1–5. Routledge, London

Norton, B.G. (1991). *Toward Unity Among Environmentalists*. Oxford University Press, New York

Princen, T & Finger, M. (1994). *Environmental NGOs in World Politics*. Routledge, London

Chapter 1: The scope of conservation

Adams, W. et al. (2004). 'Biodiversity Conservation and the Eradication of Poverty'. *Science,* 306: 1146–1149

Belt, H.V.D. (2004). 'Networking nature or "Serengeti behind the dikes"'. *History and Technology,* 20: 311–333

Butler, D. & Merton, D. (1992). *The Black Robin: Saving the World's Most Endangered Bird*. Oxford University Press, New York

Day, D. (1987). *The Whale War*. Routledge & Kegan Paul, London

Doughty, R.W. (1975). *Feather Fashions and Bird Preservation. A Study in Nature Protection.* University of California Press, Berkeley

Earthwatch (2002). *Business & Biodiversity – The Handbook for Corporate Action.* Earthwatch, IUCN & WCSD, Oxford, UK and Gland, Switzerland

Wong, K. (2009). 'Decoding the mammoth'. *Scientific American,* January 2009, 300: 26–27

Chapter 2: The conservation movement

Carson, R. (1999). *Silent Spring.* Penguin Books, London

Conwentz, H. (1909). *The care of natural monuments.* Cambridge University Press, Cambridge, MA

Fitter, R & Scott, P. (1978). *The Penitent Butchers: The Fauna Preservation Society 1903–1978.* Collins, London

Grant, C.G. (2005). *The Remarkable Life of William Beebe: Explorer and Naturalist.* Island Press, Washington DC

Grove, R.H (1992). 'Origins of Western Environmentalism'. *Scientific American,* 247: 42–47

Holdgate, M. (1999). *The Green Web: A union for world conservation.* Earthscan and IUCN, London

Jepson, P. & Canney, S. (2003). 'Values-led conservation'. *Global Ecology and Biogeography,* 12: 271–274

Jepson, P. &. Whittaker, J. (2002). 'Histories of protected areas: internationalisation of conservationist values and their adoption in the Netherlands Indies'. *Environment and History,* 8: 129–172

Myers, N. et al. (2000). 'Biodiversity hotspots for conservation priorities'. *Nature,* 403: 853–858.

Nash, R. (2002). *Wilderness and the American Mind.* Yale University Press, New Haven, CT

Paddle, R. (2002). *The Last Tasmanian Tiger: The History and Extinction of the Thylacine.* Cambridge University Press, Cambridge

Prendergast, D.K. & Adams, W.M. (2003). 'Colonial wildlife conservation and the origins of the Society for the Preservation of the Wild Fauna of the Empire (1903–1914)'. *Oryx*, 37: 251–260

Thomas, K. (1984). *Man and the Natural World: Changing Attitudes in England 1500–1800*. Penguin, London

Trefethen, J.B. (1961). *Crusade for Wildlife*. Stackpole, Harrisburg, PA and the Boone & Crockett Club, New York

Wilson, E.O. (1984). *Biophilia*. Harvard University Press, Cambridge, MA

Chapter 3: Building influence

Agrawal, A. & Lemos, M.C. (2006). 'A Greener Revolution in the making? Environmental Governance in the twenty-first century'. *Environment,* 49: 37–45

Cashore, B. (2002). 'Legitimacy and the privatisation of environmental governance. How non-state market driven governance systems gain rule-making authority'. *Governance: An international Journal of Policy, Administration and Institutions*, 15: 503–529

Goffman, E. (1974). *Frame Analysis. An essay on the organisation of experience*. Harvard University Press, Cambridge, MA

Grimmett, R.F.A. & Jones, T.A. (1989). *Important bird areas in Europe*. International Council for Bird Preservation, Cambridge

Jepson, P. (2005). 'Governance and accountability of Environmental NGOs'. *Environmental Science and Policy,* 8: 515–524

Jordan, R. et al. (2006). 'The Rise of "New" Policy Instruments in Comparative Perspective: Has Governance Eclipsed Government?' *Political Studies,* 53: 477–496

Mace, G. (2008). 'Quantification of Extinction Risk: IUCN's System for Classifying Threatened Species'. *Conservation Biology*, 22: 1424–1442

Matthew, E. & van Gelder, J.W. (2001). *Paper Tiger, Hidden Dragons: the responsibility of international financial institutions for Indonesian forest destruction, social conflict and the financial crisis of Asia Pulp & Paper.* Friends of the Earth, London

Miller, C.A. (2000). 'The Dynamics of Framing Environmental Values and Policy: Four Models of Societal Processes'. *Environmental Values,* 9: 211–233

Oldfield, S. (Ed.) (2003). *The Trade in Wildlife: Regulation for Conservation.* Earthscan, London, Chapters 2–4 and Conclusion

Shanley, P. et al. (2002). *Tapping the Green Market. Certification and management of non-timber forest products.* Earthscan, London

Websites

(Accessed July 2009)

Birds Directive: ec.europa.eu/environment/nature/legislation/birdsdirective

Convention on Biological Diversity: www.cbd.int

Convention on International Trade in Endangered Species: www.cites.org

Habitats Directive: ec.europa.eu/environment/nature/legislation/habitatsdirective

Round Table on Sustainable Palm oil: www.rspo.org

UK Wildlife and Countryside Act 1981: www.jncc.gov.uk/page-1377

Chapter 4: Science-based conservation

Caughley, G. (1994). 'Directions in Conservation Biology'. *Journal of Animal Ecology,* 63: 215–244

Egerton, F.N. (1973). 'Changing Concepts of the Balance of Nature'. *Quarterly Review of Biology,* 48: 322–50

Frankham, R. et al. (2002). *Introduction to conservation genetics.* Cambridge University Press, Cambridge

Groomberg, B. (Ed.) (1992). *Global biodiversity: State of the earth's living processes.* Chapman and Hall, London

Ladle, R.J. & Gillson, L. (2009). 'The (Im)balance of Nature: A public understanding time-lag?' *Public Understanding of Science,* 18: 229–242

Ladle, R.J. & Malhado, A.C.M. (2007). 'Responding to Biodiversity Loss'. In Douglas, I., Huggert, R. & Perkins, C. (Eds) *Companion Encyclopedia of Geography,* 2nd Edition. Routledge, London. Chapter 50 Volume 2, pp. 821–834

MacDonald, D. & Service, K. (2006). *Key topics in conservation biology.* Wiley, San Francisco, CA

Primack, R.B. (2006). *Essentials of conservation biology,* 4th Edition. Sinauer Associates, Sunderland, MA

Pullin, A.S. (2002) *Conservation biology.* Cambridge University Press, Cambridge

Quammen, D. (1997). *The song of the Dodo: island biogeography in an age of extinctions.* Scribner, New York

Soule, M.E. (Ed.) (1986). *Conservation biology.* Sinauer Associates, Sunderland MA

Sutherland, W.J. (1998). *Conservation science and action.* Wiley, San Francisco CA

Whittaker, R.J. et al. (2005). 'Conservation Biogeography: Assessment and Prospects'. *Diversity & Distributions,* 11: 3–23

Wilson, E.O. (1992). *The diversity of life.* Belknap Press, Harvard University, Cambridge, MA

Chapter 5: Taking action

Alexander, J. & McGregor, J. (2000). 'Wildlife and Politics: CAMPFIRE in Zimbabwe'. *Development and Change,* 31: 605–627

Caruthers, J. (1995). *The Kruger National Park, A social and political history.* University of Natal Press, Pietermaritzburg, South Africa

Chape, S. (2007). *The World's Protected Areas: Status, Values and Prospects in the Twenty-first Century.* University of California Press, Berkeley, CA

Conover, M. (2000). *Resolving human–wildlife conflicts: the science of wildlife damage management.* Lewis Publishers, Boca Raton, FL

Davies, B. (2005). *Black Market: Inside the Endangered Species Trade in Asia*. Earth Aware Editions, San Rafael, CA

Hingston, R.G.W. (1931). 'Proposed British National Parks for Africa'. *Geographical Journal*, 74: 401–426

Lockwood, M. et al. (Eds) (2006). *Managing Protected Areas: A global guide*. Earthscan, London

Sellars, R.W. (1997). *Preserving Nature in the National Parks*. Yale University Press, New Haven, CT

Simberloff, D. (1998). 'Flagships, umbrellas and keystones: is single-species management *passé* in the landscape era?' *Biological Conservation*, 83: 247–257

Sutherland, W.J. & Hill, D.A. (1995). *Managing Habitats for Conservation*. Cambridge University Press, Cambridge

Websites:

(Accessed July 2009)

Indigenous Protected Areas: www.environment.gov.au/indigenous/ipa

Pumalin Park: www.parquepumalin.cl

Wildlife Trusts Living Landscapes initiative: www.wildlifetrusts.org

Chapter 6: Financing conservation

Chan, K.M.A. et al. (2006). 'Conservation Planning for Ecosystem Services'. *PLoSBiology*, 4: 379

Deacon, R.T. & Murphy, P. (1997). 'The Structure of an Environmental Transaction: The Debt-for-Nature Swap'. *Land Economics*, 73: 1–24

Farber, S.C. (2000). 'Economic and ecological concepts for valuing ecosystem services'. *Ecological Economics*, 41: 375–393

Gustanski, J.A. & Squires, R. (2000). *Protecting the Land: Conservation Easements Past, Present and Future*. Island Press, Washington DC

Pierce, F. (2008). 'Carbon trading: dirty, sexy money'. *New Scientist*, 2652: 38–41

Chapter 7: Conservation's critics

Berkes, F. (2004). 'Rethinking Community-Based Conservation'. *Conservation Biology*, 18: 621–630

Brockington, D. (2002). *Fortress Conservation. The Preservation of the Mkomazi Game Reserve, Tanzania*. Indiana University Press, Oxford

Brockington, D. et al. (2006). 'Conservation, Human Rights and Poverty Reduction'. *Conservation Biology*, 20: 250–252

Cernea, M.M. & Schmidt-Soltau, K. (2006). 'Poverty Risks and National Parks: Policy Issues in Conservation and Resettlement'. *World Development*, 34: 1808

Chapin, M. (2004). 'A Challenge to Conservationists'. *World Watch Magazine*, 17(6): 17–24

MacDonald, C. (2008). *Green Inc.* The Lyons Press, Guildford, CT

Oates, J.F. (1999). *Myth and reality in the rainforest. How conservation strategies are failing in West Africa*. University of California Press, Berkeley

Websites:

(Accessed July 2009)

Big Green. Inside the nature conservancy: www.washingtonpost.com/wp-dyn/content/linkset/2007/11/16/LI2007111600631.html

Chapter 8: Twenty-first-century conservation

Adams, W.M. (2003). *Future Nature: a vision for conservation*. Earthscan, London

Donlan, J. (2005). 'Rewilding North America'. *Nature,* 436: 913–914

Jepson, P. & Canney, S. (2003). 'Values-led conservation'. *Global Ecology and Biogeography,* 12: 271–274

Ladle, R.J., Jepson, P. & Whittaker, R.J. (2005). 'Scientists and the media: the struggle for legitimacy in climate change and conservation science'. *Interdisciplinary Science Reviews,* 30: 231–240

Ladle, R.J. & Jepson, P. (2008) 'Toward a biocultural theory of avoided extinction'. *Conservation Letters,* 1: 111–118

Nichols, H. (2009). 'Ten extinct beasts that could walk the Earth again'. *New Scientist,* 2690: 24–28

Pimm, S.L. & Raven, P. (2000). 'Extinction by numbers'. *Nature,* 403: 843–845

Roberts, C. (2007). *The Unnatural History of the Sea: The Past and Future of Humanity and Fishing.* Gaia Books, London

Sodhi, N.S. & Brook, B.W. (2006). *Southeast Asian biodiversity in crisis.* Cambridge University Press, Cambridge

Thomas, C.D. et al. (2004). 'Extinction risk from climate change'. *Nature,* 427: 145–148

Turvey, S.T., Pitman R.L., Taylor B.L. et al. (2007). 'First human-caused extinction of a cetacean species?'. *Biology Letters,* 3: 537–540

Vera, F., Buissink, F. & Weidema, J. (2007). *Wilderness in Europe.* Tirion Natuur, Netherlands

Zimov, S.A. (2005). 'Pleistocene Park: return of the mammoth's ecosystem'. *Science,* 308: 796.

Index

Note: Page numbers for illustrations appear in italics.

aboriginal Australians 91–2
Acheronian species 162–3
action plans, species 112
Adams, Professor Bill 11
advice, expert 35
advocacy 36, 39
Africa 3, 138–40, 166
  East 60
  forced evictions 137–40
  human-elephant conflict
    111–12
  South 89–90, 96
  sub-Saharan 94–6
agricultural land, restoring as
    wildlife habitats 100, 102
agriculture, historical 98
Amazon 143–4
  forest 74
America
  central and south 145
  fundraising 114, 120–3
amphibians 71
Anatolian Shepherd dogs 148
animal welfare movement 9–10
animals
  reintroducing extinct 1–2, 7
  trade in parts 108
  see also extinction
anthropology 80–1
Argentina 94

assessment schemes 42
Attenborough, David 164
Auckland University 166
Australian indigenous protected
    areas 91–2
Australian Natural History
    Museum 170

back to the future 164–6
baiji 158
banks and deforestation 48–9
bathosphere 21
bears 78
Beebe, William 20–1
Beijing's Forestry University
    158
Benfica 38
big business 145–6
'Big Green' series 145
bilateral funds 124–5
bills, Private Members' 22
biodiversity 29–30, 125
  hotspots 31–2, 76, 123
  offsets 132–3
Biodiversity Action Plan, UK
    112
biofuels 47
bioinformatics 68–9
biology, conservation 52

biophilia 37
BirdLife International 28–9,
    30, 42, 95
birds 30, 38, 41, 71, 100, 117
    Chatham Island robin 2–3
    red kite 6–7
Birds Directive 41, 42
bison 20, 94
bittern 100
black rhinos 107
Blue Planet, The
    (Attenborough) 164
Boone and Crockett Club 18,
    19–20
branding 31–2
breeding 104–6
brown bears 78
Burung Indonesia 95
bushmeat 63
businesses
    and donating 126, 128
    promoting conservation 5,
        159–61

campaigning 6, 36, 37
CAMPFIRE 109
capacity-building 44
captive breeding programme
    104–6
carbon dioxide in forests 134
carbon trading 132–3
Carson, Rachel 14, 16
categorisation schemes 42–3, 44
Caughley, Graham 52
CBD (Convention on
    Biological Diversity) 29,
    43, 112, 124, 125

CDM (Clean Development
    Mechanism) 133
celebrities 38
central America 145
certification 45–7
'Challenge to Conservationists,
    A' (Chapin) 140–5
Chapin, Mac 140–5
charter, *parc naturel régional* 90
Chatham Island robins 2–3
Cheetah Conservation
    Foundation 148
Chile 94
chimpanzees 105–6
China 157–9
Chinese Forest Ecological
    Benefit Compensation
    Scheme 132
CI *see* Conservation
    International
CITES (Convention on
    International Trade in
    Endangered Species)
    39–41, 44, 45
CITES Red Data Book 42
Cley Marsh 104
Climate Care 133
climate change 10, 37, 61–2,
    103, 154–7, 172
climate corridors 103
climate envelope 154–5
clock, extinction 55–6
cloning 170–1
clubs, élite 18–19
COICA 143
communities, effect of
    conservation 136–8,
    143–5, 147–9, 149–51

community conserved areas
92–3
companies
and donating 126, 128
promoting conservation 5,
159–61
comparison tools 45
compositionalist management
97–8
conflict between humans and
animals 109, 111–12
conservancy areas 92–3
conservation
definition 9–10
organisations 11–13, 14, *15*,
17–20, 22–7, 28–9, 30–3,
113–28
see also individual
organisations
purpose and philosophy 11,
151
strategy 27
conservation biology 52
conservation easements 129–30
Conservation International 38,
42–3, 76, 123, 124, 140,
145
and debt-for-nature swaps
130–1
extinction clock 55–6
hotspots 31–2, 76, 123
providing grants 141
conservation refugees 137–8
conservation science 51–81
consumer choices 45
Convention Concerning the
Protection of the World
Cultural and Natural

Heritage 84, 85
Convention on Biological
Diversity 29, 43, 112,
124, 125
Convention on International
Trade in Endangered
Species 39–41, 44, 45
Coordinating Body of
Indigenous Organizations
of the Amazon Basin
143
coral reefs 59
cork 99–100
corporate fundraising 126, 128
Corporate Responsibility Index
159
corridors 102, 103, 156
Costa Rica 61, 131
Council of Rainforest Nations
133
countryside, attitude 79
cowherds 99
creating standards 35
credits, carbon 133
cultural heritage 14

Daily Mirror 26
debt-for-nature swaps 130–1
decision-making 34–5
Declaration of Iquitos 144
deforestation 48–50, 55, 74,
133–4
dehessas 99–100
direct action 35
diseases, alleviating 171–2
displacement of people 136–8,
147–9

DNA 170
DNA barcodes 68
dogs 148
dolphins 158
donors 115–16, 126, 128
Dutch conservation
    organisations 22–3, 102–3
Dutch nature reserve 1–2,
    103–4, 167–8, 169
dykes 103

eagles 38
Earl, Sylvia 165
Earth Summit, Rio de Janeiro
    29, 45
Earthwatch 128
East Africa 60
East Anglia 169
ecological corridors 102, 103,
    156
ecological services, maintaining
    5
ecosystems 59–63, 73–5
    services 132–3
ecotones 57
EcoTrust 32–3
elephant family 122
elephants 105, 111–12
élite clubs 18–19
Encyclopedia of Life 68–9
endangered species 69–71
endowments 114
enforcement, strict 107
Environmental Funders'
    Network 123–4
environmental governance 80
environmental groups 22

'Environmental Inc.' 145
Environmental Investigation
    Agency 108
environmentalism 9, 16–17
environmental politics 80
ethnobotany 81
ethnographic methods 79–80
European Birds Directive 41
evictions 137–40
expert advice 35
extinction 71, 73, 170–1
    causes *53*, 53–6, 60, 61–2
    definition 65, 72
    reintroducing mammals 1–2,
    7
extinction clock 55–6
extinction debt 162–3

farmers and predators 148
farmland 100, 102
Fens 100, 169
feral tahr 106
finance 113–34
financial institutions and
    deforestation 48–9
fires 102
fish 60, 63, 163–4, 166
Flora and Fauna International
    19
fogging *67*
football clubs 38
Footpaths and Commons
    Preservation Society 22
Ford, Harrison 38
forests 74, 95, 133–4, 146–7,
    157–8
    fragments 57

Forest Stewardship Council
(FSC) 46, *47*
fortress conservation 136–46,
147–8
foundations 123–4
fragmentation of habitats 56–7
framing issues 35, 36, 37–8
France 90–1
Friends of the Earth (FoE) 48–9
frogs 71
functionalist approaches 102,
103–4
fundraising 114–15, 117–26,
128

Galapagos giant tortoises 72–3
game reserves 94–5, 96
game wardens 107
Gardiner, Adrian 96
gazetting 85, 87
GEF (Global Environmental
Facility) 125–6
genetic drift 64, 65
genetic engineering 7, 72–3,
156, 170–1
giant ground sloth 170
global protected area planning
frameworks 76–7
golden toads 61
Goodall, Jane 108
Google Earth 165
Gordon and Betty Moore
Foundation 123, 124
governance 88–96
governments 23–5, 124–5,
141–2
grants 123–6, 141–2

grazing 98
Great Fens Project 100, 169
green carbon standard 134
Green, Inc. 145–6
Greenpeace 37, 146
greenways *155*
guidelines 44

habitats 53–7, 59–60, 61, 70,
73–5, 154–5, 156, 162
management 97–100, 102–4
Hampstead Heath 22
hardwoods, tropical 45
Hawaiian Crow 72
HCVF (High Conservation
Value Forest) 47
health 171–2
heathland 99
Heck cattle 167
herbivores 167–8
Hierarchy of Human Needs
150, 151
high net-worth individuals
(HNWIs) 121–2
Himalayan tahr 106
Holborne, Stephanie 103
Holland 22–3, 102–4, 167–8,
169
hotspots 31–2, 76, 123
HSBC (Hong Kong and
Shanghai Bank) 128
human–nature relationship
13–14
human–wildlife conflict 109,
111–12
hunting 18–19, 62–3, 163–4
Huxley, Sir Julian 23, 26

IBAs (important bird areas) 42
ICBP (International Council
    for Bird Preservation)
    28–9, 30, 41, 42
Important Bird Areas of Europe
    42
inbreeding depression 64–5
India 111
indigenous groups 136–8,
    143–5, 147
indigenous protected areas,
    Australian (IPAs) 91–2
Indonesia 48–9, 95, 110, 117,
    125, 146–7
industry and conservation
    159–61
interdisciplinarity 77–81
intergenerational equity 17
intergovernmental organisation
    23–5
Intergovernmental Panel on
    Climate Change (IPCC)
    154
international organisations
    23–7, 28–9, 30–2
International Union for the
    Conservation of Nature
    and Natural Resources *see*
    IUCN
International Union for the
    Protection of Nature
    (IUPN) 24
Internet, for fundraising 122–3
interview as technique 79
invasion paradox 60
IUCN 24, 26, 27, 65, 71, 144
    protected areas categories
    86–7

Red List categories 69–70,
    72

Jurassic Coast World Heritage
    Site 85
J. Walter Thompson 128

Kerinci-Seblat National Park
    125
key biodiversity areas (KBAs)
    43
keystone species 62–3
Knudson, Tom 145
Konic pony 167
Kruger National Park 89–90

Laffoley, Dan 164–5
Lake Victoria 60
land
    agricultural, restoring as
        wildlife habitats 100, 102
    buying 22–3
    donating 120–1
    and easements 129–30
landscape management 103–4
laws for species conservation
    107
legacies 120–1
linkages 156
Lister, Paul 94
Little Mangere Island 2
living landscape initiative 103
lizards 67–8
lobsters 166
local people

engaging with 149
excluding 136–8, 143–5,
147–9
logframe 127
London Convention for the
Protection of African
Fauna and Flora 19

Maasai 3
MacArthur Foundation 123
MacDonald, Christine 145–6
magazines for members of
organisations 118
mammals 1–2, 3, 71, 158,
167–8
Marine Bill 82
marine conservation 163–6
Marine Stewardship Council
46
Marker, Laurie 148
market research 78–9, 117
marshes 104
Maslow, Abraham *150*, 151
matching funds 116–17
medical conditions, alleviating
171–2
medicinal plants *79*
Members of Parliament, bills
22
membership of organisations
117–20
Meso-American corridor 156
metapopulations 58
militarisation of conservation
108
Millennium Development
Goals 126

mining companies 6, 134, 157
money 113–34
Moore Foundation 123, 124
MPAs (marine protected areas)
166
multilateral funding 125
mycologists 67
Myers, Norman 31

Naardermeer 22
Namibia 92–3
National Geographic 165–6
national parks 84, 89–91
National Parks and Access to
the Countryside Act 83
National Trust 23, 79
nature and human relationship
13–14
Nature Conservancy 120–1,
130, 131, 140, 145, 146
nature reserves 1–2, 7, 94–5,
96, 103–4
Natuurmonumenten 22–3
NCA (Ngorongoro
Conservation Area) 3
Negotiated Indirect Cost
Recovery Agreement 116
Netherlands 1–2, 22–3, 102–4,
167–8, 169
Netherlands Antilles 166
New Zealand 106, 166
New Zealand Wildlife Service
2–3
NGOs 93, 95, 108, 110,
140–1, 142–6, 160
criticisms of 151–2
financing 114–31

Nicholls, Henry 170
Nicholson, Max 27
Nielson 117
Nile perch 60
non-governmental
    organisations *see* NGOs
Norfolk Wildlife Trust 104

oceans 163–6
offsetting 132–3, 134
off-site preservation 106
oil companies and conservation
    projects 6
one-horned rhinos 107
Oostvaarderplassen reserve
    1–2, 104, 167–8, 169
'open spaces' movement 22
orange roughy 163–4
organisations, conservation *see*
    conservation: organisations
overheads 115–16

palm oil 47, 146
Pan-European Ecological
    Network (PEEN) 156
Paper Dragons, Hidden Tigers
    48–9
paper parks 87
paper pulp 48, 160
Parliament, Private Members'
    bills 22
patrols 107
people
    engaging with 149
    excluding 136–8, 143–5,
        147–9

phase shifts 59, 60
Philip, Prince *25*
Philippines 109
philosophy of conservation
    151
Planet Ocean Initiative 164–6
plantation companies 47,
    159–60
plants, medicinal *79*
Pleistocene Park 168–9
PNR (*parcs naturels regionaux*)
    90–1
policing 107
policy, framing 37–9
political ecology 81
population decline 53–4, 55–8,
    64–5, 70, 172–3
population viability analysis 65
postal code analysis 119–20
poverty 110
predators 148
pre-industrial land management
    98
primate rehabilitation centres
    10
primates 10, 105–6, 162
*Principles and Guidelines on
    Indigenous and Traditional
    Peoples and Protected Areas*
    144
priorities 76
Private Members' bills 22
private reserves 93–5, 96
process-oriented approaches
    102, 103–4
project managers 127
Project Seahorse 109
proposed protected areas 85

protected areas 82–96, 156
public campaigns 6–7
public payment schemes 132
publications for members of
    organisations 118
pulp companies 48, 160
Pumalín Park 94
purpose of conservation 151

questionnaires 78–9

rainforest deforestation 38, 95,
    158
rangers 107
rare species 99, 107, 158
    birds 2–3, 6–7, 100
    extinct in the wild 72
    fish 60, 163–4, 166
    off-site preservation 106
    reintroducing 167–9
recreation-based conservation
    172
Red Data Book, CITES 42
red kite 6–7
REDD (Reduced Emissions
    from Deforestation and
    Degradation) 133–4
Red List categories 69–70, 72
reforestation 133–4
refugees, conservation 137–8
regulations 41
reintroduction 104–6
relationship-building 35
remote sensing 75
representation principle 24
reptiles 67–8, 71, 72–3, 108

reserve managers 101
reserves 88–96, 99, 100,
    102–3, 167–8, 169
resource companies 6, 134,
    159
restricted funds 114
re-wilding 167–9
rhinoceros 107
Rio de Janeiro Earth Summit
    29, 45
river dolphins 158
rivers 103
Roberts, Callum 163–4
robins, Chatham Island 2–3
Roosevelt, Theodore 18
Round Table on Sustainable
    Palm Oil (RSPO) 47–8
RSPB (Royal Society for the
    Protection of Birds) 95,
    100, 104, 119–20
rural development work
    149–51
Russia 7, 168–9

Saba 166
SACs (special areas of
    conservation) 85
Salmon Nation 33
SANParks 89
Schuster, Dr Stephen 7
science 20–1, 51–81
Scott, Peter 25, 26
seahorses 109
seal, PNR 90
seas 163–6
'Serengeti behind the dykes'
    1–2

Shamwari Game Reserve 96
shops promoting conservation 5
Sierra Club 32
Silent Spring (Carson) 14, 16
Singapore and extinction 55
site managers 101
sites of special scientific interest (SSSIs) 83–4
slaughter, unnecessary 3–4
sloth 170
snappers 166
soccer clubs 38
social anthropology 80–1
social sciences and conservation 78–81
social values *15*
Society for Conservation Biology (SCB) 52
Society for the Preservation of Wild Fauna of the Empire (SPWFE) 18–19
South Africa 89–90, 96
South America 145
Spain 99–100
SPAs (special protection areas) 41, 85
species 56–7, 66–73
    Acheronian 162–3
    extinct 1–3, 71–3
    introducing 6–7, 59–60
    keystone 62–3
species action plans 112
species–area relationship 54–6
spiny lobsters 166
standards, creating 35, 134
Stockholm Conference on the Human Environment 16–17
strict enforcement 107
Studland Bay Nature Reserve 99
sub-populations 58
sub-Saharan Africa 94–6
Sumatra 47, 48–9, 95, 107
summit, Rio de Janeiro 28
supermarkets promoting conservation 5
surveys 78–9, 117
sward-grazing 98

tahr 106
taiga 168
Tanzania 3
Tasmanian tigers 170
Tawharanui Marine Park 166
taxonomists 66–7
Technology, Entertainment and Design Prize (TED) 2009 165
temperatures 154
Tenerife 68
Teso Nilo 49
Thomas, Professor Chris 61–2
thylacines 170
timber 45, 48–50, 157–8, 159–60
Titchwell Marsh 104
toads 61, 71
Tompkins, Douglas 94
tortoises 72–3
trade in animals 108
travel and offsetting 133
treaty on conservation 19

tropical forests 74, 95, 158
tropical hardwoods 45
trustees 121–2
trusts 123–4
Turner, Ted 94

UK Biodiversity Action Plan
112
UK funding 123–4
UK Wildlife Trusts 103
UNEP (United Nations
Environmental
Programme) 27, 125
UNESCO World Heritage
Convention 84, 85
*Unnatural History of the Seas,
The* (Roberts) 163–4
unrestricted funds 114, 115,
116, 117–28
US Environmental
Investigation Agency 158
US funding 123–4

values, social *15*
Vera, Frans 167
vertebrates 71
Victoria, Lake 60
Victory, eagle 38
voluntary contractual
arrangements 132
volunteering 117

wardens 101, 107
Washington Post 145
well-being 171–2

wetlands 22–3
Wetlands International 110
Which Guides 45
Whitley Fund for Nature 123
WildAid 108, 128
wildlife
conflict with humans 109,
111–12
protecting 18, 39–41, 103
restoring agricultural land as
habitats 100, 102
Wildlife Conservation Society
(WCS) 20, 116, 145
wildlife rangers 107
Wilson, E.O. 37, 55
Wilson, Robert W. 116
wine bottles 99–100
wood 45, 48–50, 157–8,
159–60
woolly mammoth 7
World Bank 125
World Commission on
Protected Areas 88
World Conservation Parks
Congress 138
World Conservation Strategy
27
WWF Portugal 38
WWF (World Wide Fund for
Nature) 47, 99–100, 134,
140, 144, 145, 146
and APRIL 49
creation 25–7, 28

Zimbabwe 109
Zoological Society of New
York 19–20

A Beginner's Guide to History of Science

9781851686810
£9.99/ $14.95

Sean Johnston weaves together intellectual history, philosophy, and social studies to offer a unique appraisal of the nature of this evolving discipline. This book demonstrates that science is a continually evolving activity that both influences and is influenced by its cultural context.

"Lucidly and engagingly written ... Johnston has managed to cover an impressive range of material, making it readily accessible to newcomers." **Patricia Fara** – author of *Science: A Four Thousand Year History*

"Clearly written without being patronising, this is a first-rate introduction to the history of science! " **Dr Peter Morris** – Head of Research at the Science Museum, London

SEAN F. JOHNSTON is Reader in the History of Science and Technology at the University of Glasgow. He is also a Fellow of the Higher Education Academy with a prior career as a physicist and systems engineer.

Browse further titles at
www.oneworld-publications.com

A Beginner's Guide to Philosophy of Science

Geoffrey Gorham considers explores the social and ethical implications of science by linking them to issues facing scientists today: human extinction, extraterrestrial intelligence, space colonization, and more.

9781851686841
£9.99/ $14.95

"Lively, accessible, and clear-headed. Good for the beginning student and for anyone wishing guidance on how to start thinking philosophically about science."
Helen Longino – Clarence Irving Lewis Professor of Philosophy at Stanford University

GEOFFREY GORHAM has been teaching and researching philosophy of science for 15 years, and is currently Associate Professor of Philosophy at Macalester College in St. Paul, Minnesota.

Browse further titles at
www.oneworld-publications.com